LOOK BEYOND TODAY

Also by Rosemary Brown
Unfinished Symphonies
Immortals at My Elbow

LOOK BEYOND TODAY

Rosemary Brown

with Sandra White

BANTAM PRESS

NEW YORK · LONDON · TORONTO · SYDNEY · AUCKLAND

TRANSWORLD PUBLISHERS LTD
61–63 Uxbridge Road, London W5 5SA

TRANSWORLD PUBLISHERS (AUSTRALIA) PTY LTD
26 Harley Crescent, Condell Park, NSW 2200

TRANSWORLD PUBLISHERS (NZ) LTD
Cnr Moselle and Waipareira Aves, Henderson, Auckland

Copyright © Rosemary Brown 1986
Published 1986 by Bantam Press,
a division of Transworld Publishers Ltd

British Library Cataloguing in Publication Data
Brown, Rosemary
  Look beyond today.
  1. Mediums—Great Britain—Biography
  I. Title
  133.9′3   BF1283.B7/

ISBN 0–593–01041–8

Printed in Great Britain by
The Bath Press, Bath

CONTENTS

INTRODUCTION

Rosemary Brown is a pleasantly spoken, smartly dressed widow in her sixties. There is nothing remarkable or eccentric about her appearance. Her red brown hair, beginning to grey, is worn in a loosely waved style; her grey eyes, behind thick-lensed glasses, are candid and direct. An active member of her local Anglican church, a representative of the International Society of Soroptimists and the National Council of Women, she lives in a South London maisonette where the walls of her comfortable sitting-room are hung with an eclectic collection of pictures executed by and given to her by artist friends.

She shares the maisonette with her children – and a beagle named Bella. Rosemary will inform you, calmly and matter-of-factly, that she took over the dog from a family who could no longer cope with her *on the advice of her mother*. Bella is five, and Rosemary's mother died in 1961.

And the pictures on the walls? One, a gift from a friend, is a lovingly observed head-and-shoulders pencil portrait of Rosemary in characteristic pose: head turned slightly to one side and tilted, as if listening intently to something unseen. There's a charcoal sketch of flowers crammed into a jug, the style of which looks vaguely familiar. Rosemary will describe it lightly as 'my Van Gogh'. She drew it 'under inspiration'. And above the marble mantelpiece is a cluster of miniatures. There's something familiar about the subjects of these, too. It's impossible to mistake the leonine features of Ludwig van Beethoven, or the more refined, classically handsome profile of the young Franz Liszt.

But if the casual observer can find something of interest in these portraits of long-dead composers, Rosemary Brown looks upon them fondly as mementoes of some of her best and dearest friends, with whom she is in constant touch. For she would define herself as a 'sensitive', someone whose advanced psychic gifts of clairvoyance and clairaudience enable her to see and hear the spirits of people long departed from this world, but very much alive in the next.

Sceptics will no doubt sneer at this point, and Rosemary is, sadly, no stranger to criticism. But the story of her life and work is a remarkable one and in the 15 or so years since the first BBC documentary on her was broadcast, she has continued to arouse interest and speculation. A glance at her collection of press clippings will reveal that in just one year articles about or interviews with Rosemary appeared in publications as diverse as *Psychic News*, *Morning Star*, *News of the World*, the *Sunday Times*, *Woman's Realm*, the *Listener*, and many other publications both here and abroad.

Judging from the tone of most of the articles, many who came to mock finally wrote in much warmer terms. The *Guardian*, for instance, announced, 'Unlike so many mediums, Rosemary Brown exercises a continuing fascination and not just for those converted to an etheric way of thinking.' The London *Evening News* described her as 'enigmatic', a description which still makes her giggle, and the *Sunday Times* championed her as 'the remarkable South London lady. Mrs Brown is a seemingly ordinary middle-aged woman who treats her phenomenal psychic facility like a minor social curiosity: in no time at all you find yourself drawn into this strange world of communion with the long dead . . . she could, of course, be a straightforward, honest-to-god fake but anybody who has ever met her is able to dismiss that notion after two minutes.' The *Daily Mirror* referred to her as 'the baffling housewife from Balham', and the *New Statesman* rather faintly praised: 'Of Mrs Brown's sincerity there can be no doubt, and she has impressed many.'

The famous photographer David Bailey was one of the many people Rosemary *did* impress, and he summoned her to a photographic session, free of charge. The resulting portrait appeared in British *Vogue*, together with Bailey's prediction: 'I think we'll be hearing a lot more from Rosemary Brown.' He was right!

In the first volume of her autobiography, *Unfinished Symphonies*, Rosemary describes her life until the early 1970s, and the beginning of her role as secretary and amanuensis to a group of classical composers.

Rosemary's early life was not easy. She grew up in a household where money and, it seemed sometimes, affection were in short supply. The family house was in Balham, and even after her marriage to her husband, Charles, Rosemary continued to share the house with her mother as Charles's earnings as a freelance journalist were too precarious for them to be able to afford a home of their own. Sadly, in 1961, within months of each other, both Charles and her mother died, leaving Rosemary with two young children to support unaided. That she succeeded against the odds is a tribute to her courage and tenacity.

It was at this point that Rosemary had her second meeting with Franz Liszt – her first had been a fleeting glimpse of him as an unnamed spirit when she was a child of seven. Liszt introduced Rosemary to a group of a dozen or so classical composers with a very particular purpose in mind. Rosemary was to take down new works, which would be immediately stylistically recognizable as the works of the Masters, in order to prove to a sceptical world that there is life – and work – after death. In *Unfinished Symphonies*, Rosemary describes in detail the process by which she has brought to the present day over 600 new pieces of music from composers such as Liszt, Chopin, Schubert, Beethoven, Bach, Brahms, Schumann, Debussy, Grieg, Berlioz, Rachmaninov and Delius. Two recordings of the music have been made and released, and Rosemary herself has funded and arranged a series of concerts in reputable venues such as the Queen Elizabeth Hall, the Purcell Room, and the Wigmore Hall, as well as in many less famous musical centres.

She is in fact no stranger to the treadmill of public appearances – occasionally on stage, playing some of the composers' work, or, sometimes, as the subject of often remorselessly sceptical newspaper, television and radio journalism. With a second volume of memoirs published – *Immortals at*

My Elbow – she has travelled extensively to promote her work, despite the fact that she really prefers to lead a quiet, retiring life among family and friends.

Her work with the composers has brought her under much fire indeed, from musicologists in particular, but as well as the inevitable brickbats and denunciations she has received some heartwarming testimonials to her integrity and worth.

In his foreword to *Unfinished Symphonies*, for example, Mervyn Stockwood, then Bishop of Southwark, describes his own interest in psychic research, and his first meeting with Rosemary at a dinner in Knightsbridge organized by *Psychic News*. It was a very large affair, attended by several hundred people, who were stimulated and entertained by a remarkable concert of new music from the classical composers, performed by Rosemary herself. The Bishop had no difficulty at all in accepting that 'on the other side of the grave we discover life in another dimension with enhanced powers. If this is so, it is also reasonable to suppose that artists will continue to develop their particular gifts. Indeed, it would be a curious concept of the next world if those who had struggled creatively while they were here were not to be given the opportunity to practise their crafts.' He found nothing odd in the composers' choice of Rosemary as their means of communication, for 'the heroes in the Old and New Testament were distinguished by their integrity, not by their birth or possessions'.

Further corroboration of Rosemary's integrity and, indeed, of her mental stability – although she had not realized at the time that it had ever been in question! – was given by Professor Doctor W. H. C. Tenhaeff, after long and exhaustive clinical interviews and tests at the Institute of Parapsychology at the State University of Utrecht in Holland in 1971. He stated that of the numerous subjects he had studied and interviewed in the course of a great many years, Rosemary was one of the most interesting, reliable and level-headed. He did not feel that the often advanced theory of cryptomnesia (unconscious plagiarism) convincingly explained the origin of her compositions, and revealed that his colleague, a psychiatrist with many years' experience of asylum patients, 'was unable to find a single mental aberration, neither did our psycho-diagnostic examination give reason to conclude any deviation whatsoever. Meanwhile, plans are under way for a continued investigation in which musicologists of repute will take part. . . .'

Unfortunately for Rosemary, although many scholars have indeed examined her music, professional reticence has too often prevented musicologists from publicly according her their support. But, equally, she has been pleased and proud to receive the corroborating testimony of several eminent musicians and musicologists. Humphrey Searle, the composer and acknowledged expert on the works of Franz Liszt, was a friend and supporter until his death, as is Ian Parrott, Professor of Music at the University of Wales. She also numbers among enthusiastic advocates John Lill, Peter Katin, Tamás Vásáry and Howard Shelley.

In *Unfinished Symphonies* there is an account of how, in 1969, the BBC came to film Rosemary at work, receiving a short piece from Liszt. Geoffrey Skelton, the programme's presenter, was impressed with the piece's air of authenticity, and it was later entitled *Grubelei*. Professor Parrott finds the piece particularly satisfying – a useful weapon in Rosemary's constant battle against the sneers of the sceptics. 'It is not, on the one hand, a pale imitation of Liszt's early manner,' he writes, 'nor, on the other hand, is it utterly unlike anything he ever wrote. It is something in between; rather like the sort of experimental composition that he might have written, had he lived longer in this world. . . . Rosemary's work may remain controversial for some time, but I, for one, am prepared to back it.'

But if Rosemary's chief claim to fame is her work with the composers, it is not her only one. Her communication with the spirit world is not exclusively confined to classical composers but extends to members of her own family, for instance: to her mother, who died in 1961 at the age of 81 but with whom she has kept in more or less constant touch since; to her father, a morose and rather introverted man with whom she did not get on very well in this world, but now a close and valued companion in spirit. She has even met and befriended her maternal grandparents, who died long before she was born.

She is also in touch with many celebrities from the spirit world. John Lennon, for instance, has visited her frequently, and given her some new songs; Diana Dors and Alan Lake have passed on their direct knowledge of what happens to suicide cases in the next world; Bertrand Russell and George Bernard Shaw have gone on – and sometimes on – with messages for the next world to set us thinking.

In addition Rosemary has helped to solve problems connected with the performance of an opera first performed professionally more than 30 years after its composer died in a Nazi concentration camp – by consulting the composer himself. She has also experienced many semi-mystical encounters in spirit with revered and holy men. She has found it a great source of joy and wonder to be able to meet and befriend spirits from the next world whom she could never have known as people in this one, for, as she says, here we can only meet our contemporaries but in the next world there is no time barrier. In the words of her friend and advocate, Mervyn Stockwood, 'There is a world beyond this one, and, if we did but know it, we live out our lives in the shadow of eternity.'

Rosemary is that rare being, a person for whom the shadows have parted to allow the occasional glimpse of the brilliance beyond. Here, in her own words, are accounts of some of her amazing encounters which have produced the distilled wisdom and observations of some of the foremost names of our own and other times. Separated from them by the accidents of fortune and time, Rosemary Brown is now pleased to number them among her friends.

EARLY DAYS

I don't think about the past very much – I think we should concentrate on the present – but I do remember the first time I saw Franz Liszt. I was about seven years old, lying wide awake in bed in an attic room in the family house in Balham, South London. He appeared to me, I subsequently realized, in the cassock and flowing white hair of his later years as the Abbé Liszt after his great love, the Princess Carolyne von Sayne-Wittgenstein, had failed to obtain the Church's blessing on her divorce and he turned to religion for consolation. I had been accustomed since I was very small to seeing spirits, so the sudden appearance beside my bed of an old man in a long black robe did not scare me at all.

Liszt didn't tell me his name, but he did tell me he was a composer and pianist and that he would return later in my life to give me music. He was true to his word. Today he is the leader of a group of about twelve classical composers – which includes Chopin, Rachmaninov, Berlioz, Debussy, Beethoven, Schubert, Schumann and Bach – who come into my home and dictate new compositions to me.

They can do this in one of several different ways. Either the notes are dictated to me by name – which can sometimes be difficult as B, C, D, E, G all sound pretty much the same – as if I were some sort of musical secretary; or they try to project a picture of the score into my mind; or sometimes my hands just seem to move over the keyboard of my piano, obviously guided by whichever composer is working with me at the time. They seem to be able to use my hands as if they were a pair of gloves, to be put on at will. Usually, nowadays, the music is dictated. While the process of dictation is going on, I have no idea at all how the piece will sound in performance. Sometimes, if a piece is technically beyond me, I may have to wait to hear it until a professional musician performs it.

The composers have transmitted very many new works to me. I now have over 600 pieces of music – concertos, symphonies, even an unfinished opera – in cardboard boxes, drawers and cupboards around my flat. The object of the composers' passing on new works in this way is not simply to give the world further compositions, but to show, by passing on music that is unmistakably theirs, that there is life after death.

I was an impoverished widow with two young children when Liszt kept his promise and returned to give me music. The work involved has been tremendous. I have had a very limited musical education, which meant at first that I knew no more than the rudiments of musical notation, or how to set about orchestrating a piece. While learning all this, I have had the sometimes arduous task of keeping in contact with spirits from another world. Why they chose me for this purpose, I will never know.

I was brought up and, indeed, spent the greater part of my life in the Dickeson family home in Laitwood Road, Balham. When I was born, this was a relatively prosperous, middle-class suburb of South-West London. Our home was a solid, three-storeyed redbrick affair, with sharply pointed gables to the front. It was in the attic bedroom of this house that I had my first encounter with Liszt.

The house was built by my paternal grandfather, a master-builder, responsible for many similar houses around the area. Upon his death, and that of my grandmother, before I was born, it was left in trust for the benefit of my parents, Frank and Beatrice (commonly known as Bea), who became life tenants. They couldn't sell the house, of course, and in time it seemed as though they were tied to it.

My father suffered throughout his life from weak ankles. I remember that he always had to wear strong, high-sided support boots. He was the thirteenth of fifteen children, and he didn't seem to have much luck in life. He was apprenticed as a builder, but often, because of his poor health, couldn't get work. In those days, of course, there was no unemployment benefit to fall back on. In the First World War, he was classified C3, even towards the end of the war when so many previously rejected men were called up, so I think there must have been more wrong with him than we children realized. He was given reserve work as a telephone operator, but after the war things were pretty tight again, and my parents had to survive on the income from a single-storey hall that my grandfather had built on to the back of our house. It was let out for various functions – wedding receptions, dancing classes, boy scout meetings – and my mother would do the catering for them, making lemonade with lemonade powder, and baking biscuits and cakes.

She had a lot of courage, my mother. She was hardworking, industrious, and tried to make the best of things. But in my early days she was struggling against the odds to clean and maintain a large Victorian house single-handed, bring up three children, and help my father. She had very little time to give us the sort of loving attention that children want, and until I reached my teens my mother was always a rather remote figure, always working – either as a nurse, or helping my father run his business of hiring out the hall behind our house. I believe now that she did love us; it was just that hers was a generation brought up not to show their feelings.

When she was young, my mother hardly knew one end of a broom from the other. My maternal grandparents, David William and Emma Jane Sugg, were relatively prosperous during her young days. They were a clever family, the Suggs, obtaining their money through engineering and inventing. My mother's early life was that of a lady, with servants to do the cooking and cleaning, and no shortage of funds. But something happened – I don't know what – and the family money was lost. The rest of my mother's life was pretty much pinching and scraping to get by.

On the wall of the living-room in the maisonette where I live today is an enlargement of a photograph of my mother – a pretty, serious-faced girl in a simple white blouse and graceful long skirt, taken while she was on her honeymoon at Bexhill. And this is how I see her in the next life, I am glad to say; she has the abundant golden hair and graceful hands of her childhood, quite unlike the white hair and hands crippled with arthritis of her later years on earth.

When I was in my teens, I met my maternal grandparents for the first time. They had both died many years before, but one night my mother and I were in the scullery – the small back addition to many old-fashioned kitchens – when I saw a pleasant-faced lady enter the room and stand with us. I told my mother, 'Oh, I can see your mother', for the lady had told me who she was. At first my mother didn't believe me; didn't want to, I suspect, though she herself had some psychic gifts and occasionally 'saw' herself. But I was able to give her so much evidential detail, first about my grandmother, then about my grandfather who appeared later, that finally she *did* come to believe that her parents were alive on the other side. I think it was a source of great comfort to her to hear that they were watching over her struggles in this life.

I have never been on the same terms with my paternal grandparents. I don't know why. Perhaps it's just because in any spirit communication there has to be some point of contact, character similarities or shared interests, between the spirit and the sensitive on this earth. I suspect I just don't have enough in common with my paternal grandparents to make me receptive to them.

I don't know what sort of child I was – a little horror, I expect – but early photographs reveal a skinny, rather pretty child with bobbed hair taking part with a will in some amateur dancing display. Bobbed hair! As a small child, no more than three years old, I had very long hair indeed, so long that I could almost sit on it. One day I got beneath the dining-room table with a pair of scissors and chopped off a section of hair at the side of my face. I don't know why! My hair was my father's pride and joy, and my poor mother didn't know what to do for the best. She tried to level things up by chopping off some hair from the other side but it looked so odd that in the end she was forced to take me to the hairdresser, who first bobbed, then crimped my hair into sausagey curls with a pair of old-fashioned curling tongs that used to burn if they touched the skin of your neck or face.

My mother waited in trepidation for my father's reaction to my new hairstyle, but he was always a morose, rather unobservant man. When he saw me that night, he didn't remark on my hair at all. Finally, in desperation, my mother asked him, 'What do you think of Baby's hair?' (As the youngest of three children, and the only girl, I was always known as Baby.) 'Oh, it looks very pretty. Much better than usual,' was his only reply.

Of my two brothers, Adrian, the eldest, now lives in retirement on the South Coast. But Eric, the middle child, and the brother closest to me in age and interests, died tragically at the age of 15 as the result of an accident at school. Some of his classmates were larking about one day, and fell against his desk, sending a heavy wooden desk lid crashing down on his unprotected skull. He was knocked forward into the desk and hit his nose hard on the bottom of it. At first it wasn't realized how seriously he had been hurt, but over the course of the next four years he slowly deteriorated until at the end he was little better than a vegetable. He could do nothing for himself, not even hold a cup. My mother and I had to do absolutely everything for him. I was just eight when he was first injured and nearly twelve when he finally died.

The death of my brother and friend, the boy with whom I used to delight in games of Islands – hopping from one piece of furniture to the next to avoid the shark-infested 'sea' of the floor – or Jungles, in which we imagined all sorts of strange and terrifying animals, left a void in my life. But children have few inhibitions about matters of the spirit – they haven't yet learned to distrust and suppress their instinctive beliefs. When my brother died, I used to go off on my own into an empty room and say, 'Eric, I know you must be there somewhere. Come and talk to me if you can.' And he did, not as the sick boy we had nursed for the last few years, but as my former playmate. I could see and hear him quite clearly in spirit, though I missed him terribly in life.

Some time after I had seen Liszt for the first time, I got the notion into my head that I would like to learn to play the piano.

I realize now that this was the reason for his first appearance: to put the idea into my head so that I'd be prepared for my later task in life. But I don't think Liszt had fully taken into account the poverty-stricken existence my family led. I pestered my parents so much that eventually they scraped together some money for piano lessons, and a man who played the piano for a ballroom dancing class in my parents' hall was hired to teach me. I don't think he knew too much about music, to tell you the truth, but he taught me a few chords and how to vamp a bit. My mastering of the pianoforte wasn't helped by the fact that our old instrument had many notes missing!

Eventually, my parents realized they were wasting their money and sent me instead to a proper teacher in Tooting Bec. I had to go to his home for the lessons, which meant I actually got to play on a piano with all its notes, although I still had to practise at home on our old dud of a piano. Apart from that, there was another problem. Our piano was kept in what we called the sitting-room, which was only used on the rare occasions when we had visitors. There was no electricity in our house, and no heating except for a coal fire in the living-room. The room where I had to practise was illuminated by two gas brackets, which cast only a dim light. In the winter, trying desperately to practise in this dark, draughty, totally unheated room, I can remember crying bitterly because I wanted so much to play but my fingers were so cold and stiff that I could hardly move them. It meant, of course, that I didn't practise as much as I should have done. And, in any case, the piano lessons were short-lived. We were always a poor family, and, when times got even tougher, it was the piano lessons that went first.

In my teens, I did odd jobs and saved money for piano lessons, but even they only lasted two terms and when war broke out they had to be dropped. My last series of piano lessons was for a year from 1951 to 1952 before I married. My husband and I met after he returned from Egypt, a widower. He was Charles Philip Brown, son of Thomas William Brown, who had been Minister for Horticulture in the Department of Agriculture in King Farouk's Egypt. Charles had spent part of his working life as a journalist, and was an expert on Middle East affairs. But bad times were set to follow me through life; the income of a freelance journalist is at best precarious, and my husband and I could not afford to pay for piano lessons for me. Once again, they were a luxury which had to go.

And that is just about the measure of my musical training – or lack of it. But I think Liszt's early appearance instilled in me an interest and receptivity to music which I maintained despite the setbacks to come.

It always amuses my friends – in this world – when sometimes we switch on the radio and I'll say, 'That's Schubert! No, it's Mozart. Or is it Beethoven?' All these great composers have dictated new works to me but I still haven't got the ability or the talent to recognize one from the other cold. I have the greatest admiration for musical pundits such as Joseph Cooper or Robin Ray who can name from a brief musical excerpt not only the composer and the piece, but sometimes even from which movement the 'quotation' has been taken. It always comes as a great surprise to people when they discover I can't play many of the works I have received. They are far too complicated for someone with my basic technique. But I think it's fair to say that I would recognize one of *my* pieces, or, rather, a piece I had transcribed, if I were suddenly to hear it, unannounced, on the radio or in concert.

It was actually in March 1964 that Liszt and I started to work together. It came about as a result of a curious chain of events which, without my realizing it at first, was totally to change my life.

When my husband died at the end of August 1961, I was left penniless with two children, aged 8 and 4½, to bring up unaided. It was also the middle of the school holidays, which meant there was no question of my finding a job as there would have been no one to look after the children. I applied for National Assistance and was allocated £4 1s 6d a week to keep the three of us until my widowed mother's allowance came through, and when it did I was not allowed the full amount as my husband's cards had apparently been incorrectly stamped. It was essential to get a job. I tried to get some kind of secretarial work that would fit in with school hours, but there was nothing going. There was, however, a job in the school kitchens. Even though it was poorly paid, I thought myself lucky to get it.

I had been working in the school kitchens for about three years when I had an accident. It was my turn to wash the dining-room tables after lunch when I slipped and fell on a piece of carrot which one of the children must have dropped. As I fell, I caught my ribs a glancing blow on the corner of the table, and was knocked unconscious. I was taken by ambulance to the South London Hospital in Clapham, where my midriff was put in plaster because of two broken ribs, and my arm in a sling. And all because of a piece of squashed carrot!

I was off work for weeks with instructions not to do any housework. I read, and I knitted, and, one afternoon, feeling bored, I sat down at the piano. It was that afternoon that Liszt appeared very vividly, standing beside me. And instead of finding a piece of music and playing it myself, I found that Liszt was guiding my hands. Music was being played by me without any conscious effort on my part; music I had never heard before. After that afternoon, he kept coming back and giving me more and more music. He seemed to be able to take over my hands as easily as putting on a pair of gloves.

After several of these dreamlike afternoons, Liszt said I must write down the music. With my limited musical knowledge, the work was painfully slow. But we built up a good working relationship. He was patient and understanding when I failed to take down a piece correctly because it was too difficult for me, and he would repeat the notes over and over again until I got it right. Once we had perfected our dictation technique, he began to bring the other composers to me. As time passed by, I became the surprised possessor of hundreds of new works, which deserved a wider audience. But how could I get them to the public?

By word of mouth, a correspondent on the *Daily Telegraph* and a reporter on BBC's *Woman's Hour* heard something about my music, and both wanted to interview me. Then I was invited to give a lecture-recital at Sutton Young Spiritualists' Church. Peter Dorling, a BBC television producer, got to hear of it and asked me to do a television documentary about my work. After that I was off!

When Liszt first came to me, many years ago, he told me that my life wouldn't be easy. I was used to poverty, coping alone with hardship, trying to survive, but I could never have guessed that an ordinary housewife from South London was destined to become world-famous. In the next few years I was to travel widely, giving lectures and recitals, taking part in television programmes and radio broadcasts, telling thousands, even millions, of people about the music. My first volume of autobiography, *Unfinished Symphonies*, has been published in many countries, including France, Holland and America, all of which I visited to help promote the book.

It sounds glamorous, I know, but on promotion tours you're not given time to draw breath. As soon as your feet touch the ground in front of a publicity person you're whisked off to a succession of studios and press receptions. It can be very wearying, and not enjoyable at all, but of course I do want to help publishers to sell my books so the effort is worthwhile.

An interesting point about travel is that, of course, spirits do continue to appear to me, even in transit. I've sat beside a spirit in an aeroplane, for instance. And as in the next life there are no boundaries of time and place – everywhere is here, and here is everywhere – Liszt, Chopin, even my mother, continue to appear to me even on my travels.

I'm quite blasé about television and radio appearances now. They tend to go in bouts. There's a recital of the music, or publication in paperback of one of my books, and a fresh cycle of interest begins. I've been on *Start the Week* with Richard Baker twice, aided and abetted by Liszt. I was invited on to the *Russell Harty Show* once, and made the mistake of telling all my friends to look out for me on it, and even bought a new dress that cost more than I could really afford in readiness for my appearance. And then, at the last minute, the programme's researchers decided that someone else was more sensational than me, and I was dropped. Which just goes to show that I'm not always blessed with a useful premonition!

I've also appeared on chat shows in France, Holland and Ireland, and in New York on David Frost's programme there, and the famous *Johnny Carson Show*. Not bad for a housewife and mother from Balham! But I've never made it on to *Wogan*, and I'd love to meet him.

There was a rather amusing postscript to my last appearance

on the BBC. It's quite common knowledge – at least in the BBC post room – that the Irish singer Dana's real name is Rosemary Brown. From time to time I will receive a collection of letters, forwarded to my address by the BBC, only to discover when I open them that they all begin something like: 'Dear Dana, I do love you. . . .' There must be something more than usually musical about the name Rosemary Brown!

But there have been setbacks to my work, too. In some circles I have been regarded as an eccentric, or even as a freak. I was, for instance, put through rigorous psychiatric tests by Professor Tenhaeff and his associates at the University of Utrecht in Holland – which I'm pleased to say I passed with flying colours! And some of the cheap journalism on the subject of my work with the composers has been positively libellous.

At first there was a great deal of curiosity about the music – I think there was always the underlying belief that I would be exposed as a charlatan and then everything would go on as before. But no one – despite numerous tests under stringent conditions – has been able to label my music fraudulent in any way, and that fact in turn has brought about a backlash of resistance from people who obviously see me as some kind of challenge to their expert status. But I have never wanted to be either a concert pianist or a musicologist. I'm quite untrained for such work, and am happy to work quietly in the background with the composers and the countless other spirits who visit me.

Some eminent musicologists have admitted to me in private that they *do* believe in my work, but that they dare not risk admitting it in public. A few – and to them I am deeply indebted – have been brave enough to risk academic ridicule and adverse publicity by declaring their conviction that the music transmitted to me is genuinely from the composers named. For Professor Ian Parrott's personal opinion of my work, see Appendix 1.

I have had to hire halls myself and pay professional musicians to play the music in order for it to reach a wider audience. Some professional musicians, jealous of my work, have refused to play it even though offered their usual fees. Sometimes I take part in recitals myself, but only to play the more simple pieces. When Philips decided to make a record of the music – alas, it is no longer in their catalogue – it was a professional musician, Peter Katin, who recorded the pieces. But they did let me play a few things on the 'B' side.

It's tremendously hard work, and an expensive business, organizing these concerts. I've organized musical events in a variety of venues but it's important to reach the recognized centres of excellence such as the Wigmore Hall and the Purcell Room. But what with the soloist's fee, the hire of the hall, advertising and programme printing, the cost of these events can be crippling. I fund the concerts by going without, spending my savings, even selling things, but still I almost always run at a loss. I suppose I'm just not very good at the business side of things, but I do feel that concerts are a very important way of getting the music heard by the public.

Just for the record, royalties received by me for the publication of the composers' new music have been minimal and, owing to an accounting mix-up, so far I have received the grand sum of £100 in royalties from the release of a second record of the music by a German company, Intercord. Unfortunately, the recording is almost impossible to obtain in this country, except through the costly procedure of ordering it specially from a record shop with an export labels side. For those interested in ordering the record, its catalogue number is Intercord 160.819, and its title 'Musikmedium Rosemary Brown'.

Nevertheless, my work has brought me into frequent contact with a wide range of talented musicians, mainly pianists. I am proud that artists of the calibre of Peter Jacobs, Peter Katin, Howard Shelley, John Lill and Cristina Ortiz have all played the music I have transcribed. And this year Rhonda Gillespie will be the soloist at a concert of new music by Beethoven, Liszt, Schubert and Chopin at the Queen Elizabeth Hall. (The Liszt piece is a short celebration of the centenary of his birth, and the Beethoven piece is a new piano sonata which will be receiving its première.)

Many other eminent pianists believe in my work, but won't risk playing it for fear of being ridiculed. Indeed, one prominent performer told me he could not play my music for fear of being labelled mad. I wonder what that makes *me*? But all too often musicians are not well off, may perhaps have a young family to support. I don't blame them for being reluctant to take a chance but equally I doubt that the public would be put off them if they did. I think that most people are genuinely intrigued by the music rather than annoyed by it.

The concert pianist John Lill has bravely spoken out in favour of my work. Sometimes, when he's appearing as a soloist with a famous orchestra, a player will call out in rehearsal: 'How's Beethoven, John? Have you seen him lately?' This kind of remark – and I've certainly had my share of them, too – can be very hurtful even though I, and the people who perform the music, have grown accustomed to them.

It seems sometimes as though my life has been one long struggle. As if it isn't hard enough getting the music from the composers, I have the even harder task of bringing it to people's attention and convincing them that it's genuine. For almost 21 years I have been battling to reach an audience. When Liszt began his work with me, while we were both still awaiting my début, he warned me that to undertake this task would bring much suffering to me. 'Remember,' he said, 'you will be doing battle, not just for us but for God and humanity. It is a desperate attempt to bring peace and enlightenment to the human race. Many will scorn you, even your own friends may turn against you, but we will never fail you. When you are belittled, do not lose heart, for the strong arms of God are beneath you to uphold your soul.' Since then, I have been the butt of ridicule for the ignorant and the learned alike. Friends have proved false and deserted me. Human nature has proved more frail than I had ever expected. Liszt has remained my greatest help and comforter during the bad times, and has generously praised my small successes. And it is because of him that I have come to write this book.

The music was originally sent to convince people that there is a life after death, but after so many years on that tack I'd like now to approach things from a different aspect. Perhaps if I can convince people that there is a life after death, not only for composers but also for the actresses, singers, statesmen, philosophers, scientists, authors and other public figures, as well as the countless ordinary people I have also been privileged to

24

meet in spirit, then they will believe in the music.

This is a book to set you thinking. I hope it will answer some questions, clear up some myths, and help you to reach some conclusions of your own. Who knows? At the end of it you might believe in something new, whether it be the music or the fact of life after death. It doesn't matter which. The two are part of the same glorious whole.

LIFE AFTER DEATH

If only we all had eyes to see what I see, and ears to hear what I hear! But perhaps this would only complicate life for some people, and others would be scared. I think, in fact, that thousands of millions of people all over the world *do* share my psychic gifts to a greater or lesser extent but don't acknowledge or display them as they are too afraid of being greeted with disapproval or disbelief. I've noticed in my reading, however, that attitudes to these gifts vary considerably from country to country and society to society, with some of the less 'developed' societies taking a considerably more liberal view than so-called 'advanced' ones.

Perhaps at this stage I should explain a little about the various psychic processes to which I refer in this book. I am, for instance, commonly referred to as a medium; this is someone who is used by spirits as a means, or medium, of communication. Although in this broadest sense I could be said to provide a channel of communication for the spirit world, the word 'medium' today has come to be used more commonly to describe the work of practitioners such as Doris Fisher Stokes, a lady I admire tremendously for her courage throughout illness, and for the help and comfort she brings to so many people. But Doris Fisher Stokes's style of mediumship is to conduct 'platform' work, the dispensing of messages at random to some members of a vast assembled audience. I know that she will also undertake individual psychic consultations, and that her gifts have even been of use to the police in conducting murder investigations or searches for lost children.

My own use of the processes of clairvoyance (the seeing of spirits) and clairaudience (hearing their voices) is generally conducted in a much more private way. I do not, for instance, perform platform work, give psychic consultations to members of the public for a fee, or belong nowadays to any psychic circle. I restrict my psychic work – the passing on of spirit messages, for instance – to my immediate family and friends. This is because I find that the work can be very taxing physically, and I have never been someone who is at ease while performing some psychic function before a large audience. Apart from that, I believe I should concentrate on writing out the new musical works of the composers in the 'hereafter' – a full-time job in itself.

Clairvoyance, the sighting of spirits, is in no way a frightening or 'ghostly' occurrence. To me, the spirits who appear are as unthreatening as any corporeal visitor, and like them they will sit chatting on the sofa or stand casually by the piano while I play. Clairaudience, the hearing of spirits, often accompanies clairvoyance, although the two processes are not necessarily interdependent. Generally speaking, the voices I hear are not 'in my head' – though that is not totally unknown. Usually the sound of a spirit voice comes from the mouth of a spirit when clairaudience is involved, or from the direction of that spirit. There are subtle differences between spirit and normal human voices, but occasionally they sound exactly like the person in the flesh. (I have, for instance, heard my own husband Charles's voice sounding exactly as it did in this life, but I think that on that occasion he was making a really enormous effort to be sure I heard him clearly.) Sometimes the voices are crystal-clear; sometimes they are muffled or faint, as though at the end of a bad telephone line. This is why I can't always be certain that I haven't made a slip while taking down some music or a message from, say, Bertrand Russell, whose vocabulary is far wider than mine.

I also have some experience of spirit healing, and there is a later chapter on this subject. But I must restrict this work to my family and circle of friends too, as it can be immensely draining and there are so many sick people in this world that it is impossible to treat more than a few.

I am not a Spiritualist. It is noticeable that there are alarmingly sectarian and anti-Christian attitudes among the advocates of Spiritualism. I am a dedicated and practising member of the Anglican Church, which means more to me than anything else. This rules me out of Spiritualism. Like most people who have studied the Bible at great length, I do not take it literally, word for word – aiming instead to follow its general precepts and teachings in my daily life. I have had many mystical experiences and my personal encounters with Christ have confirmed my acceptance of Christianity.

I often receive premonitions, or tip-offs, from the spirit world that something will happen, either to me or to a friend or acquaintance. I don't set out to delve into the future, but if I can help somebody by passing on a timely message about what the future may hold for them, I am happy to do so. Not everyone is happy to receive a message in this way, of course. I would certainly not pass on a communication to a nervous or sceptical recipient unless it was a matter of life or death. Fear of the unknown is a natural thing which is bound to grip us all at some time or other. But when we know more about life after death, when we realize it's a wonderful reality, let's hope that fear of death, the fear of the actual transition and of what is to come, will be wiped out for all of us.

Once, I remember, the spirit of a recently passed-on man appeared and I listened to him clairaudiently as he bemoaned the fact that his wife now regarded him as some kind of bogeyman just because his physical body was dead. 'Can't she realize,' he asked me, 'that I am still the same person, and that I love her just as much? If only she didn't shrink from the thought of me, and think of me as a mere ghost! I am real, I am alive, I am the man she knew and loved.' I tried to explain to the man's wife or, rather, widow. She said she understood what I was saying but that it was difficult to visualize her husband as a living human being. 'Tell him,' she begged me, 'that I am trying to understand. It is just that he does not seem to be there. But I do believe there is another life, and I do still love him.'

This seemed to console the man's spirit. 'I'll be waiting for her when she comes over,' he said, 'and I'll be watching over her until then. Tell her she always *did* need watching.' I repeated all

28

this to the lady, and the bit about her always needing to be watched obviously meant something to her because she laughed out loud. She explained, 'He always used to call me a flirt, but I wasn't really. I just liked to be admired. He used to say: "I'm watching you." You have made me feel he really is alive. I shan't feel he is just a wispy ghost now.'

I know there *is* life after death, but I also understand only too well how some people find it difficult to accept that there is life beyond this world, and how the very thought of such a thing can make them uncomfortable. I, of course, accept it because I have grown up with the knowledge of life after death, a knowledge instilled in me through my personal experiences.

However, there have been times when 'proof' has arrived to convince me still further in the most startling way. I think you will agree with me that it is strange to see the spirit of a dead person beside his or her grave. Still more strange to see one standing beside his or her own coffin at their funeral service! Yet this is what happened when my father died.

He had asked, long before his death – in fact, before he was taken ill – to have his body cremated. I don't think he minded the idea of his body being buried but he had a belief that his soul would be freed all the more quickly from his body if cremation took place. So, according to his wishes, my mother and I arranged for a cremation service.

I stood beside my mother, trying to comfort her during the brief service. Although she herself sometimes 'saw', I think she was too overtaken by her natural grief to notice that my father was standing right beside his own coffin. Rather surprised to see him at his own funeral, I gazed at him, transfixed. 'What's the matter?' he asked. 'You look as though you've seen a ghost! I'm not a ghost, I'm your father.' I was a bit taken aback because it sounded as if he did not realize he had passed over, but his next words made things clear. 'As for that,' he said, pointing to the coffin, 'blow that! Thank God I'm out of that old body at last.'

I was relieved to see that he knew he had passed on and felt no qualms about the disposal of his body. He told me he had come to be near my mother and to try to cheer her up, and he confessed that it gave him a lot of satisfaction to see his outworn body, which had given him so much suffering, being 'finished off', as he put it!

During his life my father had to wear support boots because of his weak ankles. He had always yearned for a pair of patent leather shoes, and to have clothes like a real 'toff'. We were too poor for him to have anything other than one working suit, and another cheap suit for best. But when he appeared to me after passing over, he was dressed in a beautiful Savile Row type suit and shiny black patent shoes. His wish had come true at last! He told me to write and tell my brother Adrian what he was wearing, and said he would show himself to him in the same outfit. My brother was serving in Burma at the time, with the Royal Signals Corps. He wrote to me to say that he knew our father had passed on as he had seen him. Our letters crossed in the post – each of us having written to the other with identical details of our father's appearance after reaching the other side.

My brother has some degree of psychic ability but wisely keeps very quiet about it, as he sees no reason to endure the jibes of disbelievers. Like me, he is a regular church-goer, and I sometimes think he feels his church would frown on such abilities. But if you have them, you can't disown them. You just can't help being made that way. Of course, they are not wrong in themselves. How can abilities God has given be wrong? I regard them as gifts of the spirit, to be used wisely and well.

And isn't it strange to reflect how the whole of the Bible, both the Old and the New Testaments, is full of stories of the supernatural? Of visions and voices, of prophets and angels, hundreds of happenings that defy, or appear to defy, natural law? And yet the emergence today of anything that hints at the supernatural is often frowned upon, and those people connected with the supernatural condemned by narrow-minded bigots. But the same sceptics can accept, lock, stock and barrel, all the events related in the Bible and never turn a hair! Nor is it entirely logical that some branches of the Christian churches – not all, I am glad to say – should be so inimical to the idea that the spirits of the dead can appear in this world. After all, from time to time, in desperate cases, a service of exorcism is performed by the Church, so they must acknowledge the existence of evil spirits. Why not, then, of good ones?

My husband, Charles, wasn't psychic, but he did not

condemn my abilities. In fact, he was sympathetic and very interested in extrasensory perception. Through me he was to become convinced of the life hereafter, and resume a loving relationship with his mother.

His mother, Minnie Ethel Archer, had died when he was a very small boy of seven or so, but he remembered her clearly and with great love. He once took me to see her grave in Tunbridge Wells, and I could see that even though many years had passed, her departure was still a great loss to him. He had one sister, Georgina, who died during the war; we named our own daughter after her. He had been very attached to his sister, and felt her passing as another great loss. He also had two brothers in the world of the spirit: one who died as a child from diphtheria, and another, Tommy, who died during the Second World War in Japanese hands.

So the greater part of his family was already in the world of spirit, and after we married I began to see all those 'dead' relatives of his: his mother, father, brothers and sister. They sent frequent messages to him, often filled with vital details of an evidential nature. Charles began to feel he had not lost them, that they were merely unseen to him. I still see some of them now – I saw his mother a few weeks ago, for instance. She's like a second mother to me, with her pleasant round face and big dark eyes which reveal her Italian blood.

The most amazing of these communications for my husband were the messages from his first wife. He rarely spoke of her to me. It was a great tragedy to him when she died very young, and he told me that he had never expected to marry again. But she herself, on her deathbed, had told him he would, and that he would find happiness and have a family.

One night, when our two toddlers were fast asleep, I was sitting up with Charles, who was having a very bad night. In the last years of his life he was very ill indeed with non-alcoholic cirrhosis of the liver. His first wife appeared to me then and throughout her subsequent visits I found her to be a very sweet-natured person, not in the least bit jealous that Charles was now married to me. In fact, she often said she was very grateful to me for caring for him and making his life happier. Surely this shows that she had a very real love for him.

Anyway, on this particular occasion she appeared with a youngster of about 17 standing by her side. I told Charles that she said the boy was their son, but he remarked, 'We had no child.' She asked me to remind him of a miscarriage she had had, and which he had in fact forgotten. The baby, she said, had entered the spirit world and grown up there. She added that she had named their son Mark Antony. At this, my husband roared with laughter. He said that he had loathed the name ever since he had had to learn the whole rôle at school. His former wife knew about this and often teased him, saying if they ever had a son she would call him Mark Antony.

So my husband was the father not only of our two children but of a third, previously conceived child. He adored our own, in the same way that they adored him, and he must have been very sad at having to leave them in this world. But I like to think he must have been greatly consoled by the reunion with his first wife and their son whom he could now see for the first time. He later worked out the age Mark Antony would have been had he lived on in this world, and said he would indeed have been about 17, the age I estimated the boy to have been. My husband's first wife's appearance with the news of their son, whom up until then I had known nothing about, helped to deepen his faith in my ability to receive messages from the other side.

Children seem to accept these things much more matter-of-factly than adults. They still question, of course – perhaps more so – but they have open minds, not yet swayed by biased thinking. After my husband passed over, he would always manifest himself if either the children or I were ill, making a special effort to show that he was still watching over us. I believe that after his passing he was particularly close to our son Thomas for quite some time. Thomas was not even five years old when his father 'died', and yet I would find the little boy making all sorts of repairs about the house when things broke or went wrong. 'How did you know how to do that?' I would ask him. And he would simply state, 'Daddy told me.' And then there was the night when we were all watching television and my husband started switching the light on and off. I think he was trying to prove to the children that he was there. They were delighted. 'Ask him to do it again,' they kept saying. My children grew up fully accepting that, although their father had gone from our world, he had just passed over to a better place, to wait for us all to join him there.

Adults, on the other hand, can take a lot of convincing. I don't really try these days to convince people against their will. And, sometimes, if I'm with someone and a spirit gives me a message for them, I think twice before passing it on in case they think I'm slightly mad. Passing on messages can be a very wearying and time-consuming business. You can't just say to someone, 'Your mother has a message for you. She says. . . .' You often have to give all sorts of details about his or her mother before you can get the message accepted.

Sometimes, though, these bits of evidence present themselves when you least expect them. My daughter Georgina witnessed one such occasion one afternoon a few years ago when she was present at a meeting between myself and Julia Jones, a scriptwriter for the BBC who had come to interview me in connection with a play to be based on my life. Miss Jones questioned me about my background, as one would expect, and a while later I told her that I could see a spirit woman in the room. She was clearly curious, so I attempted to describe the spirit to her, detailing the colour of her hair, her eyes, height and build, etc. But Miss Jones seemed to lose interest, saying she could think of no one who answered that description.

And then I told her that the spirit lady had injured one of her hands in this world. She told me that in this life it had not healed properly, causing her considerable pain across the palm of her hand if she tried to open it flat. My daughter Georgina has described the effect of this information: 'It was startling. Miss Jones's mouth dropped open and all colour drained from her face – clearly the shock of recognition. When she recovered, she explained who my mother had seen.' Apparently, Julia Jones had been hoping I might contact her mother who had died a short time previously. When the description of the spirit visitor did not fit her mother, she was disappointed. But at the mention of a hand injury, she immediately thought of an old friend who had died many years previously who exactly fitted the description, which was fairly specific.

33

This is not the first time Georgina has been present when such things have happened. Indeed, she has occasionally seen spirit visitors at the same time I have – a very rare occurrence. But, in the main, my children, in common with so many other people, have so far chosen not to develop or use their psychic powers. I am not unhappy about this, and have always told them, 'Don't feel you've got to do anything.' They are both involved in supremely practical professions: Thomas works for a bank, and Georgina is now studying nuclear physics.

Because I now accept all the strange things that happen to me as perfectly normal, I sometimes forget that most people need some kind of proof that I *do* have the abilities that I claim to have. As I have said, I try not to get into situations where I feel obliged to summon up some sort of contact and demonstrate my gifts in an evidential way. It's always on those occasions when you are trying hardest that things can turn out rather unconvincingly. In my experience, the most convincing episodes have all happened completely spontaneously and – sometimes – without my understanding at all what was going on. Often I have been left in the dark as to the full meaning of the communication until some time later when all is revealed. Here I want to talk about a few episodes which stand out in my mind as particularly convincing.

I have a friend, Else, in Hamburg whom I have known for some years. When I first got to know her, about 1975, her mother was still alive, although I never met her. But shortly after Else's mother passed on, I began to see her. At first I didn't know who she was, but she was speaking in German and I only knew a few words then, so her identity wasn't very clear to me at all. Fortunately, Liszt arrived to do some translating, as he so often does. Through Liszt this lady said that she wanted to send a message of love and thanks to her daughter, who had taken care of her during her last illness.

Then she went on to tell me about a little silver shoe that had been of great sentimental value to her. I think it had something to do with her wedding day. I got the impression it was the sort of tiny silver shoe that you see on the top of wedding cakes. The lady went on to tell me that the shoe was among her possessions and her daughter would find it one day. So I wrote to Else and described the shoe in detail and told her that her mother wanted her to find it. She wrote back to say she had gone through her mother's possessions and hadn't found the shoe; also, she had been unaware of its existence. But a few days after that I received another letter, telling me that she had at last found the shoe, exactly as I had described it, but that it was gold, not silver. I thought: Oh, well, you can't win them all. Slight slip-up there! Liszt said there had obviously been some sort of confusion but this was definitely the shoe Else's mother wanted her to find.

More than a year later, Else decided to take the shoe to be cleaned. When the jeweller did so, he told her that it wasn't gold but silver! It had been coated with some kind of 'gold'. Else wrote me an excited letter, telling me that I was right, Liszt was right, and she was convinced by this episode that her mother was indeed alive in the hereafter and communicating through me. It could not have been telepathy because Else did not know about the shoe and I thought at first that I had made a mistake about the metal. I have always thought that this is a very good example of the accuracy of spirit information, made more outstanding because it was all done at great distance, with letters flying between England and Germany!

Another of my favourite examples also concerns Germany, and my son, Thomas. A student of modern languages at Jesus College, Oxford, he went to Hamburg in 1977, to work as a language teacher in a grammar school. I had never met the Jungs, a family living in Hamburg, but Thomas contacted them via an introduction from Fiona and Humphrey Searle in London. Later, Thomas was to write:

> I knew all along it was a musical family as Herr Jung is a skilled amateur cellist and organizer of a regular subscription series of chamber music recitals in Hamburg. However, I obviously did not get to know every detail of their family history at once, although I knew that Herr Jung's brother, who lives in Rüdesheim, was also a great music-lover, and that their parents had been friends of several notable musicians of the inter-war and post-war years, including the celebrated pianist Walter

Gieseking. Gieseking died in the mid-1950s but his name had occurred in conversation with the Hamburg Jungs soon after I had met them.

Just after Christmas 1977, when Thomas was at home for the holidays, a gentleman appeared to me in spirit. He was of stocky build and announced himself to be Walter Gieseking. He told me that he had known the Jung family in Rüdesheim very well, having been a frequent visitor to their house. This, he said, would be evident from their Visitors' Book for the period. He described the Jungs' Rüdesheim house as a place where he could be himself – which was how Thomas had felt among the Jungs in Hamburg. Gieseking told me that as a party piece he would play variations on 'Chopsticks'. And he went on to give some personal details about the Jungs which I later confirmed with Thomas. At no time prior to this had my son made any mention of the Jung–Gieseking connection to me.

The remarkable sequel to this story came in spring 1978, when Thomas was again a guest at the Jungs' Hamburg flat. Herr Jung showed him the present which his brother had recently given him: a copy of their parents' Visitors' Book, chronicling the immediate post-war years, as mentioned to me by Gieseking himself. Leafing through the facsimile pages, Thomas saw that on virtually every day when there were visitors' entries, Walter Gieseking's signature stood prominent among them. Thomas had not been particularly impressed at the time by my visit from Gieseking, but this later corroboration of his message about the Visitors' Book was incontrovertible proof of my genuine communication with him.

On another occasion, Peter Dorling, a BBC television producer, was making a television programme about me and asked if I could provide some background information which wasn't readily available to the general public to help prove the authenticity of my sources. I asked Liszt for his help and he made the telling point: 'If it is something that is in a book, people will say you have read it. But if there is no record anywhere, it can't be checked.' Nevertheless, a few days later he came back and told me he thought he could provide some evidential details. He informed me that in 1854 he had been to

Leipzig and had been taken ill while he was there. He was attended by a certain Doctor Richter and thought this might be worth mentioning.

The first reaction from the BBC was that it could not be true. Liszt, they said, had given up touring in 1848 and so was unlikely to have been in Leipzig at that late date. Fortunately, Peter decided to go on delving. In an obscure work of reference, the sort that you wouldn't find in just any library, he found out that Liszt *did* in fact go to Leipzig in 1854, and was taken ill while he was there.

In another incident with Peter Dorling, during lunch at his home one day, he asked me if I could get anyone from the other side connected with him. I was pretty tired as it had been a rather heavy working day but I did get a man who said his name was Alfred. I described him to Peter, but the description seemed to mean nothing to him. Some time later, when I saw Peter again, he told me the man I had seen was his grandfather. And his name was not Alfred, but Albert. Well, I did say I was tired – too tired to concentrate and register accurately!

Dorothy Bacon of *Life* magazine once brought Richard Rodney Bennett to my home because she wanted the opinion of a contemporary composer on the music I was receiving. Richard's opinion was generally favourable and as I'd enjoyed hearing him at the piano, I asked him if he were giving a recital soon which I could attend. He said he was but that he was a little worried about his interpretation of a piece by Debussy. I had no idea which piece Richard was planning to play but Debussy himself appeared and said he was delighted to learn that the recital was going to take place. He gave me detailed instructions to pass on to Richard, saying which phrases needed more pedal, which chords should be *staccato*, and so on. I had no way of knowing if this advice would mean anything, but when I gave it to Richard Rodney Bennett he said, 'Well, that's strange because everything you have said could apply to the piece of music I am concerned about. In fact, it could not apply to any other piece of Debussy's music.' He followed the advice given by Debussy and discovered it solved all his problems.

In 1981, I flew to Switzerland to stay for a short holiday with some friends, the Eisenbeisses, in St Gallen, where it just so happened that the world championship chess match between Korchnoi and Karpov was taking place. Dr Eisenbeiss, an economist, is also a keen amateur chess player who delights in conducting long-distance games with correspondents by letter and phone. I myself am in almost total ignorance of chess. I just about know the names of the pieces – mainly through crossword puzzles – but I certainly don't follow international chess.

Each move in the epic game was being relayed to my host by telex. Just after he had learned of one particular move, he came into a room where I was sitting and mentioned the state of play so far. I said quite spontaneously, 'The answer to this must be a move with the King.' Knowing that I do not play or understand chess, Dr Eisenbeiss was amazed by the authoritative tone of my reply.

He said in a letter he wrote recently: 'For parapsychologists I would like to point out that the telepathy theory cannot be used to explain this case because I had only just been informed of the move by telex and had not given any thought at all to the possible reply,' he writes. 'Also, Mrs Brown did not know what move had been communicated to me by telex, or anything about the match. It was only later that I was able to work out the best move, and it was in fact the one mentioned by Mrs Brown.'

From this incident I learned that there are such things as chess-playing ghosts! There must have been spectral spectators following the championship with great interest. And one of them, as quick as a streak of lightning, had named the move to me as soon as Dr Eisenbeiss had finished speaking. There are certainly some quick-thinking ghosts in the spirit world!

Two people, both connected with Fleet Street, have given me permission to relate further instances of spirit communication which took place quite spontaneously and unexpectedly. Journalists are usually downright sceptical of things like this and so I am delighted to have won over two of the profession at the very least into believing in life after death.

Vicki Mackenzie is now a good friend of mine. We met when she was working for the *Daily Mail* and was sent to interview me about my work. The interview was quite long as Vicki questioned me conscientiously and later wrote an excellent article which was sadly jostled out of the southern editions by more topical news.

When the interview was almost over I saw the spirit of a woman standing near to Vicki. Much that the lady had to say cannot be published as it concerns private family matters. (So often the best evidence turns out to be too personal to be made public!) I described the lady's appearance: small, dainty, with a round face and an un-English accent. She was dressed in a rose-coloured *crêpe de Chine* dress, waisted, with a camellia on the collar. The woman was saying something about a large ring with a big stone which she'd had but never worn. She was giving details, too, of some miniatures of her family. I drew the approximate size of these with a pencil and paper, and there were other messages of love and of a personal nature.

Vicki thought it sounded like her Czech aunt who had died recently. Apparently, she'd been very fond of her niece, although they had not met often. That evening, Vicki rang her uncle and questioned him. There was no way she could have known about the ring which had never been worn in her presence, and she had never seen the miniatures either. Her uncle confirmed that his wife had in fact owned two rings with very large stones which she had never worn as she felt they were too large for her small hands. And in his house there were three miniatures of his wife's cousins, each 2 inches high – exactly the size I had drawn them. These were kept in a glass case but not in a part of the house which Vicki would ever have seen. When she mentioned her aunt's dress, her uncle thought for a moment, then said his wife had worn a waisted dress with a camellia on the collar *long before Vicki was born.*

Vicki later wrote: 'Both my uncle and I were astonished and thrilled with the accuracy of Rosemary's description of my aunt and her belongings because it seemed to make my aunt come alive again, even though neither of us had seen her or heard of her since her passing. And for me, who had no knowledge of the objects described, it was the ultimate proof that my aunt had been seen by Rosemary Brown.'

Unity Hall is the women's page editor of the *News of the World.* I first met her more than 12 years ago through my work. I took to her immediately, finding her a sympathetic listener with a keen insight into the frailties of human nature. She received communications on two separate occasions. The first one took place when she and I and other guests were relaxing after dinner. I became aware that the spirit of a young man was standing beside her, with one hand on her shoulder. She couldn't feel his hand, which was just as well as it might have been a little unnerving for her! I described his appearance and she was able to identify him. Then he proceeded to give her a message that fairly took the wind out of her sails. It was a secret known only to her – and her secret it must remain, I'm afraid – but our secrets are often known to the spirit world, as this case proves.

The second time Unity received a communication was at my home, just as we were finishing a meal and taking coffee. Beside Unity stood the spirit of another man who so much resembled Stan Laurel of the comedy duo Laurel and Hardy that I very nearly began to chuckle. The spirit even had the same little quiff of hair standing up on his head! He was plumper in the face and of stockier build so I could tell it wasn't really Laurel the comedian. Having described his appearance to Unity, I then told her what he had to say.

He was her father, who had very recently passed over into the spirit world. He spoke of a number of family matters, of which I could not have known, and sent a comforting message to his wife. He came across so clearly that Unity was very moved. She faithfully passed on the messages to her mother, who naturally had been grieving and unable to sleep. Unity said that after her mother had received the messages she had her first good night's rest since her husband had died. Spirits do, after all, usually appear for some very good reason: to help, warn, or to comfort in bereavement. I do not believe that the process of reaching this world is particularly easy – at least for some spirits – so they have to want to reach someone quite strongly before they try.

This brings up the point sometimes argued by Spiritualists and the Christian faith alike that we should not grieve for someone who has passed on. This, in my opinion, is sheer nonsense. Even if we know there is life after death, even if we know our dear ones who have gone beyond the veil are near to us and watching over us, we are human and we love them, and of course we miss their earthly presence. We miss the little endearments of a shared daily life, and their company and conversation. Unless we are devoid of human feelings we are sure to feel some sorrow in exactly the same way as if close friends or loved relatives had emigrated to a distant country and we were unlikely to see them for a long time.

Actually, that isn't a bad metaphor for life after death – there is a place that exists for our loved ones when their earthly body dies. Their spirit lives on in another dimension, in a far more beautiful place than anywhere you have seen on this earth. People you love have gone from you, but they are still near, waiting for you to join them in the wonderful world – or worlds – beyond our own.

THE OTHER SIDE

P eople constantly ask me what it's like on the other side. What have I seen there?

Speaking broadly, the next world is very similar to ours, only infinitely more beautiful. My visits there took place mainly while I was a teenager, and also more recently. On these occasions I was gravely ill, my life hanging by a thread. I believe my spirit was three-quarters of the way into the next world, and I wanted to stay there, but obviously there was work for me still to do here.

In a popular women's magazine, the television actress Stephanie Beacham gave a very interesting and, in my experience, wholly accurate account of what it is like to make the transition into the next world.

> I was seriously ill and nearly died. And I believe I passed over, passed through. And if I genuinely believe that's what I did, then I have to accept that I have seen there is an after life.
> 'I saw a huge light . . . I'm afraid I even saw cloaked figures leading me. I was being led by someone whose face was human, but my attention was focused towards the brightest light I have ever known. It was completely unfrightening, inviting, and I was going.

Stephanie believes that only the realization that her small

daughters would be left behind forced her to sink back into her earthly body. She had an emergency operation and has since gone from strength to strength in her acting career so obviously it was not yet time for her to make the transition.

The famous medium Doris Fisher Stokes has had her own experiences of the other side, but the following is the account of one of the spirits who have communicated through her as to what his passing over was like: 'I woke up to find myself in hospital here. Many of my old friends were there, too. Some of them held my hands and told me very firmly that I had passed on. It's a beautiful world here with trees and flowers, and halls of music and learning.'

Occasionally, in moments of deep sleep, when I believe the spirit can float loose from our earthly body for a while, I have visited the other side and from my brief glimpses of it, I look forward to living there some day. The colours there are more vibrant, and there are more of them than we have here, including subtle in-between shades that I just couldn't describe in words. The flowers are wonderful; far more beautiful than anything I have ever seen here. Sometimes, fleetingly, I think I can catch the merest hint of their perfume, even in this world. I have seen the rolling hills of the countryside on the other side; the majestic trees, soaring mountains. Jesus said: 'In my father's house there are many mansions.' I think he was trying to tell us that there are many places on the other side; hundreds, maybe thousands of millions of them.

There are countless places in this world, too. There are different climates: arctic, tropical, dry, rainy, and so on. There are fertile countries, and barren, mountainous, flat, forested or treeless terrains. We have vast deserts and uncharted oceans. If our world is so varied, it's no wonder that the next world is, if not more so. There are also buildings of every description – libraries, concert halls, even football pitches! I mention this particularly because one man wrote to me especially to ask if there were football pitches on the other side, as heaven, he said, wouldn't be heaven without football!

Talking about football reminds me of an incident when I went to be interviewed on London's Capital Radio. There was a woman on reception whose job it was to usher me into the interview room, then out again. I kept seeing the spirit of a little boy standing beside her with a brand-new football under his arm. Dare I mention this to her? I thought. Some people can take it, and others are frightened to death! But the little boy looked so keen and anxious, and he was willing me to tell her he was there, so I took a chance.

It turned out to be her eight-year-old son who had been mad about football. They had just bought him a brand-new ball when he was killed in an accident. The lady was delighted to hear he had a replica of the ball and was getting pleasure out of it. She was so delighted, in fact, that she gave me a bottle of champagne. My news of her son came so unexpectedly, and caused her so much spontaneous joy, that I was glad I had taken the plunge.

This lady's little boy appeared to me at the age and in the pose he knew she would most associate with him. But this does not necessarily mean that he would stay eight years old for ever on the other side. People do evolve and develop there. My own mother, for instance, died with crippled, arthritic hands, white hair and decayed teeth, of which she was terribly ashamed. But on the very night she died, I saw her spirit looking about 40 years old. Her hair was golden again, her hands and teeth restored – to her great delight. Nowadays, when I see her, she looks and sounds like a girl of 20 or so. According to Liszt, this process does normally take longer with most spirits. Possibly, my mother's belief and interest in the spirit world during this life accelerated the process in the next.

On another occasion I saw the spirit of a lady who wanted me to pass on a message to a friend. To identify herself, she held up one hand and I observed aloud that the top of one finger was missing. The recipient of the message knew just who I was describing when she heard this detail, but she was horrified. 'Does that mean she still hasn't got her whole finger?' she asked in dismay. It didn't, of course. It was just another instance of a spirit choosing to appear in a way which would instantly identify her to friends in this world.

And in my own experience, of course, there is the case of Liszt, who chose first to appear to me in the guise of the Abbé Liszt, familiar from photographic studies of him taken towards the end of his life. Nowadays, when I see him, it is in the form of a handsome, smiling man in his thirties or so.

The appearance spirits will show us in this world is not necessarily how they would appear in theirs. I believe they can change their appearance more or less at will, just as we can here with skilful props and make-up. Real proof of a spirit's personality comes not so much through details of the appearance it assumes, as through its personality, its way of speaking, use of key phrases, etc.

Liszt has told me that there is a substance of a sort in the next world. To each other, those who dwell there are comparatively solid, just as we are to each other in this world. But in the next world, spirits may gravitate to different levels of consciousness, the highest and most evolved of which are formless, detectable only by a form of soul-sensing. This evolution is very gradual. There is no question of being suddenly flung from one bodily state to another of complete formlessness. This state is only achieved when a spirit has achieved an advanced state of consciousness and wishes to *be*, rather than to appear.

In the earlier stages, while a spirit still has an appearance, I believe the outward 'age' of the spirit will reflect its character. Spirits will look the age they most truly are, just as in this world there are old people who despite their years look and are perennially young. It might not be too fanciful, therefore, to believe that there is such a thing as an eternal Peter Pan; a spirit which will remain forever young.

In our world there are souls who are inwardly beautiful but who have had the misfortune to be born ugly or malformed, and the opposite is very true as well, isn't it? There are people who are outwardly beautiful or handsome, but inwardly very ugly. The great difference in the next world is that there people look exactly what they are. There, the inner soul is revealed. There is no hiding behind a pretty mask. You cannot deceive people into thinking you are something you are not.

When my mother passed on to the next plane she was able to communicate with me a great deal. We felt her presence around the house very close to us for the two or three weeks following her death, perhaps because there had been a great rapport between us and she already knew quite a lot about the next plane before she reached it. She died in a coma, and soon after leaving her physical body, 'came to' to find her own mother waiting to greet her.

Then she saw there was a nun standing nearby. The nun asked my mother if there were anything she wanted, and my mother replied that she would love a cup of tea! My mother always loved her cuppa, and obviously nothing was going to change that. But as soon as she spoke, she realized she had probably been foolish. She knew she was now in the after-life, where perhaps they didn't go in for cuppas! The nun disappeared and returned very soon, carrying something which looked like a cup of tea, smelled like tea and tasted like tea. My mother drank it, and said it was just like drinking a cup of tea in our world.

Mother told me she was surprised to find herself in surroundings that evidently had some kind of solidity. Even if things only *seemed* solid, she said they were definitely real. But, then, what is reality? It is only when we wake up that we dismiss a dream as unreal. My father had a theory, one of the many he was always forming, that it is this life which is the dream – or nightmare – but we won't realize that until we wake up in the next world.

Spirits from the next world assert that *their* world is the real one, and the world we are in is a shadowy one – that is, a distorted reflection of reality. All the same, while we are here in this world, it is real enough to us. We can't ignore it as so many people try to ignore the existence of the other side.

There isn't just heaven for the good, and hell for the bad on the other side. It isn't nearly as black or white as that. People in the next world tell me that we gravitate naturally to the plane that is most suitable to us. So, people who have been cruel or evil in this world gravitate to darker places. They go automatically, as if drawn by a magnet as a result of their evil actions. They have allowed themselves to sink to a certain level in this world, and so to that level they will go in the next. And there they will stay until they make some effort to improve.

It seems a very democratic world over there. There is hope for everyone, but for some people it will be a long journey towards the light. You can't buy yourself out of a dark place. On the other side you are appreciated for what you are, not for any wealth or title you may have had in this world. Many people get cut down to size. Those who have been truly wicked on this earth, but who genuinely wish to advance, may do so as long as they are forgiven by those who have been wronged by them. That is why the habit of forgiveness is such a vital one to acquire in this life. People cannot be released from the bondage of sin until they are forgiven – as the Christian religion so clearly realises.

One thing to remember, though, is that people don't always immediately change, even on the other side. People who have been wicked and cruel in this world are quite likely to stay that way in the next, at least for a time. That's one of the dangers of messing around with Ouija boards, trying to call up spirits. If you don't know what you are doing, you might be visited by an evil spirit, just looking for somewhere to create more mischief. I'll explain more in a later chapter about why we should not attempt to call up spirits, but, rather, should wait for them to contact us.

We can't ignore our physical bodies. They are always clamouring for attention, food, water, sleep. We *can* ignore our spiritual bodies, and certainly millions of people do, but our spiritual bodies are everlasting, and one day we shall have to live in them minus our physical bodies.

Perhaps, then, it's not such a bad idea to think about the next world in order to try to prepare ourselves for it. After all, if you were going on a journey in this world you would give it some thought beforehand. It's only common sense, therefore, to make some preparation for that final journey. Keeping an open mind on the subject of life after death could be helpful when you make the transition to the next world.

After many years in the next world, my mother says there are far too many people who arrive there without any inkling of an after-life. She has been there now for almost a quarter of a century, so she has had plenty of time to observe, and I listen intently to what she says.

People who have been taught a religion – any religion – have at least a vague idea about life after death, which helps them to come to terms with it. But my mother says lots of people are pitifully confused on arrival and can't make out what has happened or where they are. That's why there is a need for helpers on the other side. Most people are met by someone they knew in this world, like a good friend or relative. And there are many volunteer helpers like nuns and nurses who devote themselves to looking after new arrivals until they have adapted. And then, of course, there are babies and young children who will need looking after until they can fend for themselves.

Naturally, people are frightened of the unknown, and therefore frightened about the other side. But if people only realized how wonderful the other side is, they would not be afraid of going there. Throughout my life, I've had enough glimpses of the other side to convince me it's a wonderful place. I look forward to going there eventually but I want to stay here near my children for now. When the time comes to leave this world I shall travel with a hopeful heart to be reunited with my husband and parents and friends. Most of all, as a Christian, I hope one day to be with Christ.

SPIRITS

Spiritualists are sometimes accused of calling up the dead. You never hear anyone accuse the dead of trying to call us up! But this is the way it happened to me, and I believe it is the safest way.

If it doesn't happen this way for you, my advice is to leave spirit matters well alone, and not to go dabbling lightly in things that are beyond many people's understanding. The chances of a lay person managing to contact the one particular person they are seeking on the other side are pretty remote, I'm afraid, but by experimenting with Ouija boards or the apparatus of seances, you might well open up channels of communication with some really malign spirits. There are some fairly unkind people lurking on the other side so my advice to those not psychically gifted is: Leave well alone.

The majority of people in this life will perhaps never consciously see, hear or feel a spirit but it has become obvious to me, as a psychic person, that people in the next world *do* want to get in touch with us, and sometimes succeed. When Liszt first came to see me, for instance, he came of his own accord. I wasn't trying to get in touch with him. He came because he wanted to use me to pass on new works from himself and the other great composers, to demonstrate their survival, and I was happy to oblige.

And that is usually how it works with me. I wait until someone from over there wants to get in touch with me. Sometimes, perhaps when a concert of the composers' music is going to be performed and there is a query on it, I have been asked by the musicians involved to clear up the problem with Liszt. I always have to say to them that I can't guarantee I'll be able to manage it. Liszt isn't at my beck and call. Rather, I am at his. But usually he is aware that there is a problem and appears of his own accord to help sort things out.

Spirits can appear at any time and in any place – while I'm walking down the street, or sitting in my living-room, or having a meal with friends in a restaurant. Sometimes I can both see and hear them; sometimes just one or the other. I take these things in my stride, but I know that the very thought of spirits can frighten some people, usually because they have been conditioned to be afraid. Children often seem to be aware of spirits – how many instances have you heard of a child's having an invisible 'friend', for instance? – but they soon find out that their parents generally prefer them not to get involved with the supernatural, and frown on their ability to communicate with spirits.

Because of these attitudes, it's always difficult to predict whether people will be able to cope with spirit visits. Often, I'm talking to a friend and I can see someone from the spirit world standing beside them. Or I might be in a restaurant, having a meal with friends, and I'll notice a solitary businessman having lunch, impervious to the spirit sitting opposite him. I always keep quiet about it, though. After all, I could hardly approach a complete stranger and say, 'Excuse me, did you know your dead mother has been with you throughout lunch?'

I think most people are unsure about their attitude towards the supernatural. Sometimes they think they could cope with it; at others, they are not so sure. I constantly have to remind myself that many people find it strange or frightening. But, after all, people have always been afraid of the unknown. Someone flying for the first time can be apprehensive; any routine experience – such as changing schools or jobs – can bother us. I think it's just that people are naturally happier with the things they know and understand and that they are reluctant to think about, let alone investigate, new spheres.

Generally speaking, spirits are aware of our feelings towards them. In my case they know they can turn up at any time and I won't be bothered, but they won't usually appear to people they know will be afraid. Sometimes, though, they make mistakes! I had a great friend called Bunty who lived nearly opposite my own maisonette. When she died, her son, Douglas, took on the task of feeding Bunty's dog and taking it for walks. He told me that one day, while he was putting out the dog's food, he was absolutely certain he heard his mother's distinctive footsteps, coming up the hallway behind him. 'I was petrified,' he told me. 'I was standing there, shaking, saying, "Mum, please don't be there. Please don't be there!"'

I told him that Bunty was still the mum he loved; she was no different just because she was out of her physical body. He could accept what I was saying in theory, but he couldn't cope with it in practice, even though I told him that spirits usually come out of love. Bunty loved her son and wanted him to be reassured that she was all right; she just hadn't bargained on his being scared of her.

Mind you, I have to admit that even I have been startled by spirit visits once or twice. The two occasions I remember most clearly both involve my husband, Charles.

After he died, I took a long time to get over my grief. I knew he was alive on the other side, and no longer suffering on this, but I couldn't think about him without breaking down. I know there is another life, but I had lost the physical presence of the man I loved. I was alone with two young children, and I missed his companionship and conversation terribly. Even a psychic is human, after all.

One night, after my children had gone to sleep, I was sitting up in bed, reading or praying. I wasn't even thinking about my husband but purposely blocking him out of my thoughts because memories of him got me so upset. Then, all of a sudden, I heard his voice. Just one word, the name he had always called me since the birth of our children: 'Mummy.' The voice was so strong and clear, so definitely his, that I looked up and there he was, as clear as anything. I wasn't frightened, although definitely startled. But it was wonderful to see and hear him again. I thought: He's still with me. This reassured me greatly, and from that moment on I began to be able to pull myself out of my grief. I feel sure that Charles concentrated all his love and

51

concern for me into appearing at that precise time because he knew how greatly I would be helped by it.

On another occasion, he appeared so suddenly that he did manage to shake me. My children and I all slept in one room because I could not afford to heat more than one. I had bunk beds for the children, and a single bed for me. My daughter, Georgina, had been ill, and whenever that happened she liked to sleep in my bed, saying it made her feel better. So in the night she asked if she could get into my bed, and I climbed into her bunk instead. This ritual of exchanging beds always improved my daughter's health! I didn't want to go to sleep because I wanted to make sure that she was all right. I lay awake, every so often looking over at her to see that she was OK. I was just looking again to see if she had fallen asleep, which meant I might be able to get some rest, when I sat up to find my husband's face right in front of me. I was so startled I said: 'Charles, don't do that!' He just smiled and instantly disappeared. I realized afterwards that he had been as concerned for our daughter as I was, and had been keeping an eye on her in his own way.

After all, if a person has loved and protected another throughout life, that desire to love and protect does not die with them. I think this is perfectly natural. Imagine if you had passed over and saw one of your children in danger in this life. You would do your best to try to stop a possible accident, wouldn't you?

Often people on the other side try to help their friends and relatives here. Sometimes they can foresee a possible accident and try to give a warning. That is one of the things that makes me think that not everything is predestined because if an accident was definitely fixed to happen, there would be nothing you could do to stop it.

Occasionally, I have received warnings, and the ones that I can most readily remember came to me during the war. When I went home from work I always took the same route. But sometimes, if there was an air raid on, I would be told by voices from the other side not to go home my usual way. I always followed these 'hunches', and it always happened on those occasions that a bomb fell on the route I had avoided. And sometimes I've been standing on the pavement, about to cross a road, when a spirit voice has called: 'Stop! Get back.' I've done so only to be narrowly missed by a speeding car!

Spirits also come to comfort us when we are in need. A few years ago my daughter was taken ill in the night. She was sharing a flat with an old school friend at the time, and didn't want to worry or bother me by telling me how dreadful she felt. In the early hours of the morning, feeling very ill, she suddenly saw a figure beside her bed. At first she wondered, 'What is my flatmate doing, standing there in her nightdress?' Then she realized that it wasn't her flatmate, who is a very tall girl, as the visitor was only about 5 feet tall. Gradually, it dawned on Georgina that she was seeing the spirit of her own grandmother. The sense of reassurance and love which the spirit brought with her helped my daughter greatly, and she soon felt much better. I think it's lovely that my mother, who passed on in January 1961, should come back years later to help my daughter. My mother was always a very fond grandmother, and her love for Georgina and Thomas has not diminished.

Besides bringing comfort and love, spirits have also stepped in to stop me being made a fool of. Obviously, people like me are fair game for sceptics, and I don't often get interviewed by the media without their trying to catch me out in some way. After my first book was published, for instance, there was a great deal of media interest and I was invited here, there and everywhere. I found it pretty nerveracking to have to defend myself and my beliefs time and again. While I wanted people to know about the music, I felt that I was being treated rather harshly by being put into situations where I had to battle to convince people of my sincerity.

I was once invited to appear on Richard Baker's *Start the Week* on Radio Four. I was informed beforehand by Liszt that a contemporary composer who is a trained and brilliant musician would play musical pastiches in the style of various composers, and then ask me to play something too. The clear inference was that I was doing the same thing as he was, merely imitating a style.

But I am not a trained musician. I have no natural talent, no wide musical knowledge, and certainly no desire to perform party-trick pieces like 'Chopsticks' in the style of Rachmaninov. The compositions I produce are not skilful pastiches, but entirely new works which bear all the characteristic style of their composers while containing no more than the odd bar or two echoed from a previous work. I was understandably worried about this proposed ordeal but Liszt appeared the night before and tried to put my mind at rest. 'Get in first,' he said. 'Tell them you know about people who can produce music in the style of a certain composer, but they are trained musicians, whereas you are not.'

The BBC sent a car for me, but we got caught up in a traffic jam in Putney. We were stuck for over an hour, with the driver getting into quite a stew though I stayed surprisingly calm. When we eventually got to the BBC, the programme was nearly over. I was rushed into the studio where Richard Baker was already talking about my work. There was hardly time for me to do or say anything, but I sat down and did manage to say my piece exactly as Liszt had told me to. Then I went to the piano and played just a few bars of music given to me by Liszt. I didn't have time really to illustrate anything much, but I felt I'd put my case as well as I could. Afterwards, Richard Baker told me he was astonished that I was able to refute all the points he was going to make *before* he had so much as opened his mouth. He was caught a bit off-guard, just as I had feared I would be!

The spirits often do forewarn me, and tell me what to do and say on these occasions, which is a great help as I am a fairly simple person. Knowing that I have the backing and support of Liszt and the others gives me the courage to go on.

On one occasion, Liszt even came up with a 'party trick' to help me get through a very difficult encounter. I was going to be interviewed on television in Birmingham by a lady called Wendy Cooper. One of my previous books had just been published and the television people were calling in a computer expert who was going to use his professional knowledge to analyse my music and say whether it was genuine or not. Wendy herself was not a believer in life after death, I gathered, nor were the other people in the studio. People are much more open-minded nowadays, but in those early days I was often greeted with suspicion and hostility. I felt very uncomfortable but Liszt said to me, 'Don't worry. Everything will be all right.'

Just before we went on the air, the studio was very busy with technicians everywhere. I hadn't even seen a copy of my new book yet myself so I picked up the review copy which was to be flashed on screen. I looked at it, then Wendy took it back and placed it on the piano stool – they had brought in a piano because they wanted me to play some of my pieces from the composers. After putting down the book, we went and sat some distance away. There was no one near the piano at all, but I saw Liszt walk over to it and then pick up the book to have a look at the jacket. He was curious, too. He had a good look then put it down. Everyone saw the book move but they could not see Liszt lifting it up. All they saw was the book rising up from the stool, hovering in mid-air, and then sinking down again. Everyone about me was thunderstruck. I said, 'That's Liszt. He just wanted to look at the book.' From that moment on, my credibility rocketed. Everyone was looking at me in a different light, and even the computer genius declared my music genuine!

Wendy subsequently wrote an article about this in the *Birmingham Post* in which she said:

> In the past I have certainly been sceptical where the supernatural is concerned, and none of the mediums or clairvoyants I have met and interviewed has done anything to change my mind.
>
> Rosemary Brown has – or at the very least she has forced my mind open to the fact that there is something about her story and her music that defies rational explanation.

Such physical manifestations don't often happen, however. Spirits are, on the whole, considerate and well disposed. They wouldn't want to frighten or upset people, and risk turning them hostile towards psychic matters by playing scary tricks. Nevertheless I have had several experiences of spirits communicating by causing the movement of inanimate objects. On the mantelpiece of my living-room, for instance, is a set of three dark brown glass Victorian vases. These used to stand in a similar position in our family house in Balham, and on one occasion, when a school friend was particularly troubled, the tallest, central vase actually knocked three times against the wall with a loud resonant noise. Fortunately, my friend took this as a sign of encouragement rather than a frightening event.

I think that quite possibly this physical communication is hard for spirits to achieve. We know very little about how they manage to harness energy, but it may be that physical manifestations are as rare in spirit terms as the matter-defying powers of, say, Yuri Geller are in ours. I'm afraid I'm not very knowledgeable on this subject – even the ways in which television and radio work seem mysterious to me. But, interestingly, a spirit visitor has told me that it's not beyond the bounds of possibility that one day we may be able to link up with the spirit world, by using an advanced form of television. My informant tells me that it may well become possible simply to switch on our televisions and see for ourselves the spirits of people who have passed over. When that day comes, I suppose there will no longer be any need for psychics like me.

Liszt is always with me to lend support, but he is not the only one of my composers to help me out. For instance, in February 1971, when my first book was published in France, the publishers arranged for me to make a flying visit to Paris for publicity purposes. Scarcely had I stepped on to French soil when I was whisked off to start a non-stop programme of press conferences, radio interviews, and television appearances. There was hardly a moment to breathe in between the various engagements, but during a brief lull I asked Monsieur Jean Major, the publisher's representative, whether there would be time for me to visit Chopin's resting-place. 'I cannot be in Paris without going to his grave,' I said. 'Ah,' replied Monsieur Major, 'we have arranged that already. We wish to film you beside his tomb.' I was delighted to be going to Chopin's tomb but a bit put out that it was to be yet another event in the publicity round. Still, I couldn't complain. I was very lucky to be in Paris, and I appreciated very much this chance to pay my respects at Chopin's resting-place.

When the day came, we wound in slow procession through Père Lachaise cemetery, which contains the graves of so many men and women famed in the worlds of art and politics. When we reached the tomb, I found myself prey to mixed emotions. I had never thought I would have the opportunity of visiting Chopin's grave, as money for holidays and foreign travel had always been scarce.

It is a beautiful tomb, set amidst a small, lovingly tended garden plot. The monument depicts a young girl seated with her hands in her lap, her palms turned upward. Someone had placed in them a small posy of violets – Chopin's favourite flower. I suddenly felt very moved. Here lay the earthly remains of a great genius, who had died painfully young before he had had the opportunity to give the world more of his beautiful music. Thoughts of his past suffering threatened to well up and engulf me, while all the time I was dimly aware of the onlookers standing around, watching me.

What brought me firmly back to the present was seeing Chopin himself standing beside his own tomb. He smiled gently as I laid some flowers on his tomb, thanked me for them in French. 'Why do you feel so sad?' he asked. 'You know I am here and not there.' Then he pointed to his tomb. 'Ah, well, I suppose it is a grave matter,' he joked in his characteristic way. I smiled despite the sadness. Chopin was trying his best to cheer me up and support me through what could have been a very emotional situation. When I returned home to England, he gave me a new piece of music, a little nocturne, to commemorate my visit. It is a poignant piece in A minor, reminiscent of the falling of rain, or even of tears. Whenever I play it, it reminds me of that wonderful visit to Paris, and of how the composer came to cheer me up.

One of the great joys of communicating with spirit visitors has been the discovery that certain of them at least have a highly developed sense of humour. After all, the hereafter would be a pretty dull sort of place if there were no peals of laughter to be heard there. Still, I doubt that most people would believe that a visit from a spirit could be a laughing matter! In fact, I've been amused on many an occasion by a witty remark from the spirit world, and often, when I'm feeling a bit down, friends on the other side have made light-hearted conversation to try to jolly me out of the blues.

I think I tended from childhood to take life too seriously. When you grow up in a poverty-stricken household, with a father who has a morose disposition and is given to violent outbursts of temper, and a mother who is overburdened and remote, you are not likely to bubble over with high spirits. Even though I was aware of the fact that spirits on the other side were usually quite cheerful company, most of my childhood and teenage years were spent in a gloomy atmosphere. In order to survive the traumas of these years, I needed a sense of humour. And it was friends in the spirit world who taught me how to laugh.

I had an uncle who was remarkable for his courage and grand sense of humour. He was wounded in the abdomen in the First World War, and as a result was bent double for the rest of his life. Yet Uncle Joey never complained or indulged in self-pity. He was always the life and soul of any party. After 20 years of suffering, he died in the 1930s.

We all missed him terribly at our next family gathering at Christmastime. Friends and relations gathered together for a good old-fashioned singsong – and there, too, was Uncle Joey, though I doubt that anyone but I could see him. The party was going well, with everyone getting up to do party pieces. One cousin told amusing anecdotes; another was a dab hand at juggling. So far, so good. But then one of my cousins rose to her feet to sing 'The Bells of St Mary's'. Her voice would have cracked those bells had they been near! Not content with ruining one song she went on to demolish several more.

It was made even more excruciating for me because I was sitting at the front of her audience, receiving the full blast of her voice. I glanced around to see if anyone else was visibly suffering. Uncle Joey appeared, as large as life and plainly amused at my discomfort, grinned at me broadly, and said with a wink, 'Stick it, mate.' I almost burst out laughing at the funny face he pulled, but just managed to turn my giggle into a cough.

A more recent example of ghostly humour came in the form of some spirit advice to a friend who was a keen squash player. This friend had put on a lot of weight, and more than once had pulled a muscle or strained a ligament during a game. A certain wise spirit, someone I did not know in this world, appeared one day and asked me to pass on a message: 'Please tell him that if he persists in playing squash he will run the risk of recapturing the first fine careless rupture.' (Lovers of poetry will remember the unadulterated line from Robert Browning's 'Home Thoughts from Abroad' about 'The first fine careless rapture'.)

On another occasion, a few years ago, I was at a gathering where most of the guests were people who ran or frequented esoteric centres. There was one man who fancied himself greatly as a spiritual teacher. On first meeting him you could be quite dazzled by his big talk and grand manner. Deep down, however, I had my doubts about his credentials. 'Don't be taken in by him,' a spirit voice advised. 'He is a carrion-crow in peacock's clothing.' The voice was that of Sir Donald Tovey, a distinguished musicologist who passed over in the 1940s and has often communicated with me since. He has a dry sense of humour, and the ability to express his ideas fluently and vividly. The image of a carrion-crow in peacock's clothing was a very fitting one. As the evening progressed, with the young man strutting about peacock-like, I found it more and more difficult to take him seriously!

Chopin is a great wit, too, and something of a tease. I found this teasing very disconcerting at first, but when in sheer self-defence I began to tease him back he was not at all put out. 'You could not tease me unless you regarded me as a friend,' he said to me once.

He doesn't like too much formality, but on the other hand he doesn't like people to be over-familiar. And he certainly doesn't like people to take liberties with his music. He prefers his compositions to remain in the classical repertoire and not be turned into popular versions. He said to me once, rather ruefully, 'There is a danger in writing a singable tune. Sooner or later someone is sure to be tempted to write words to it. I am never quite sure whether to feel flattered or insulted when one of my compositions is turned into an advertising jingle. But it happens to us all, even the great Beethoven.'

More than once I have been asked whether the composers attend concerts of their own music – in this world, that is. I can't afford to go to many concerts, myself, but whenever I have been to a Chopin concert, he is there too. At one, a little-known pianist was playing something of Chopin's in a rather jerky style. Chopin was there, listening, with a slightly impatient expression on his face. Then he turned to me and asked, 'Why is he playing my music like a kangaroo?' Mentally, for we were in the middle of a group of rapt concert-goers, I replied defensively, 'Well, it has a kind of leaping rhythm.' 'Yes, I know, but I had something rather more delicate in mind, like a grasshopper,' Chopin explained. Somehow, I just couldn't take the rest of the piece seriously after that. When it came to an end, with a final wild jump, he murmured, 'I'm sorry I was rude about the pianist. I see now that he is very nervous. That is why his hands were springing about like startled gazelles.' So now, whenever I hear that piece, I have to chuckle at that thought of kangaroos, grasshoppers – and gazelles.

This instance also goes to illustrate that spirits can observe what is going on in our world, although in my experience this is not always the case. I think they probably have to tune in in some special way to see what is going on, and that sometimes they are not able to do so fully. For instance, Liszt may be dictating a piece of music and sometimes I have to read it back to him, note for note, as he obviously cannot see it for himself. At other times, though, he will point out a mistake by referring specifically to a particular page and line.

I've often thought that if people realized that they are being watched from the next world, they might be a bit more careful about how they behave. It reminds me of the phrase in the church service: 'From whom no secrets are hidden.' As I grew up it dawned on me, through my growing awareness of spirit, that it is possible that our every action is observed elsewhere; that our every word is heard elsewhere; that each thought we think is known elsewhere. The idea of a recording angel is, perhaps, not so unlikely.

Communication with spirits can be an awkward process, quite unlike my joking dialogue with Chopin. If, for instance, I'm receiving a message from a great thinker like Bertrand Russell, I'll be listening intently, struggling to understand, while simultaneously recording the message in writing. All too often, any interruption or questioning on my part will break the flow of communication with a spirit.

I've found sometimes that someone will be interviewing me about a certain spirit who will then obligingly turn up while the interview is going on, and begin talking to me on his or her own account. The interviewer immediately wants the spirit to stop talking to me and to answer his questions instead. A difficult three-sided conversation ensues. Sometimes, I can conduct it satisfactorily. It really does depend on the spirit involved. If it is a practised communicator, it can be quite good at answering questions in this way, but if it is only the first or second time a spirit has tried to communicate it will have the difficult task of accustoming itself to my wavelength while I am distracted by the questions and observations of a third party. It's not so easy! On the whole, the regular communicators respond better to direct questions from me because we've got to know how to work together. I have a particularly good rapport with Liszt, obviously, and more often than not he will be able to answer my questions directly.

On one occasion, Kerry Woodward, a knowledgeable musicologist and composer, held a long conversation with Beethoven through me. Kerry stated afterwards that he had no doubt at all that it was Beethoven he was communicating with, and found the experience 'fascinating'. I had received a piano sonata from Beethoven, and Kerry noticed that the *scherzo* had no dynamics. Then and there, Beethoven began to supply dynamics, bar by bar, completing them in about three minutes. And, said Kerry, they were absolutely typically Beethovian. Perhaps we were particularly lucky on that occasion, but Kerry certainly found his first-hand experience of spirit communication extremely convincing.

Generally speaking, trying to give messages to people is one of the greatest difficulties in mediumship. You're trying to listen to the spirit, then to relay the message to the sitter, and meanwhile the sitter is interrupting with fresh requests for evidence of the genuineness of the spirit messenger. If you want consistent flowing communication, it is better to let the spirit just say what it wants to say rather than to get it to answer direct questions.

Sometimes it's impossible to avoid mistakes. No medium, myself included, is infallible. All messages have to be passed through the medium's mind, which might, unconsciously, colour what is said by spirits. You will all have heard the story of the wartime message 'Send us reinforcements, we're going to advance' which ended up as 'Send us three and fourpence, we're going to a dance', after being passed from person to person. Just a few days ago I was dictating the lyrics to a new song from John Lennon into a tape recorder. I had been talking about a 'transcendental plane', but the audio-typist misheard this as a 'trance and gentle plain'. Fortunately, I spotted the mistake before it got into print, and John, who has a strong sense of humour, had quite a giggle over it.

The same sort of mistake is possible with music as well as with words. For instance, Howard Shelley, the concert pianist, and I were at a friend's house, running through a piece which had recently come from Beethoven. Howard was playing it on the piano when he stopped short, saying the music just didn't seem to follow on at that point. I had to agree, though I was perplexed. Just then Beethoven appeared and explained that when he had been dictating this piece, we had been interrupted. He didn't realize that I hadn't taken down every bar of music. It wasn't until he heard Howard play it all through that he discovered there were eight bars missing. There and then, he dictated the eight bars to me. I passed them on to Howard, bar by bar, and he wrote them in. They fitted perfectly.

On such an occasion, the spirit has appeared, unasked, for a specific purpose. My spirit visitors come out of friendship and concern, but I can never stress enough that spirits aren't always friendly. Usually, well-intentioned people will not attract a bad spirit, but if people have any serious character defect or are remiss in some way, or even if they drink heavily or misuse drugs, they can lay themselves open to bad vibrations.

Personally, I have never had that type of bad spirit contact – mainly, I think, because I lead a very prayerful life. Right from when I was a young child, I prayed a lot, and from the age of 12 I dedicated myself to the search for truth and God. I have investigated all sorts of religions, and philosophies. I started doing Yoga meditation, for instance, when I was still at school. I have followed the path of truth-seeking all my life, moving into Christian channels and devotion to Christ. I think if you lead a prayerful life, try to keep your thoughts on a good positive level all the time, then you will be on a wavelength that bad spirits can't reach. Spirits on higher levels can go down to lower levels if they choose to, to try to help the spirits there, but the lower ones can't go up any higher. It's like being at school – a teacher can teach the children, but the children can't teach the teacher. To safeguard against undesirable spirits, we should all try to lead good lives and to do our utmost not to think unpleasant thoughts.

Living a good life swathes us in light. Bad spirits live in darkness. They can't bear light, so to keep them away we need to radiate it. Bad spirits can, of course, improve with help and guidance from above, but sometimes it's a long time before they want to improve. They go on wallowing in their own evil until they cannot bear it, and decide to reform.

People often talk of mediums calling up the dead, and this is a popular myth. I don't believe any spirit can be forced to communicate with us, or summoned up at will. And surely we should not trouble the dead if they want to be left in peace? If they want to forget this world and all its traumas, then they should be allowed to do so.

Sometimes it is very hard to let go of those people we love. Just as it is hard sometimes for parents to let their children go off into the world, to live their own lives, it is hard sometimes for the bereaved to let their loved ones journey into the light, into a new life of which we on earth know so little. But perhaps it is only through being parted from our loved ones that we come to appreciate them fully. Perhaps it was only through being parted from God that we could truly appreciate Him. Perhaps that was what being cast out of the Garden of Eden was all about. Only through being deprived for a time can we really treasure what we once had. Where there is love there is a link: a bridging of space, of time and circumstances. Where there is love, an eventual reunion is completely certain. Love is the strongest force there is – St Paul was right about that – and if we let love rule all of our relationships it will bring us ultimately into harmony, and wholeness, and oneness with the supreme source of love which is God.

ANIMALS

When people approach mediums to try to contact a loved one on the other side, it is usually another human being that they are trying to communicate with. Not many people realize that animals and pets go on to the spirit world, too. In fact, one of my earliest memories is of seeing a cheetah. I was always seeing him; he seemed to trot around wherever I went. I loved him like other little girls might love a puppy.

I'm not a believer in straightforward reincarnation but in recent years I have wondered if there wasn't a connection between this cheetah and myself. Perhaps I had a link with his country in another life, or maybe someone in the spirit world who was helping me had a link with India. Perhaps it was something as simple as the fact that, as a child, I used to collect the cigarette cards from my father's packets. These would come in a series: sportsmen, trains, birds, animals . . . I remember being very impressed by the picture of a cheetah, which I thought was splendid. Maybe that early interest attracted one to me in spirit. Or perhaps someone in the spirit world may have sent him to me in childhood for company. His visits diminished as I grew older.

Later in my life, I met another big cat – also in spirit. My husband suffered from chronic asthma and spent many restless nights, sitting up in bed, giving up all hopes of sleep. To keep him company, I would sit up with him, and we would talk about everything under the sun. We had many shared interests and so there was never any shortage of subjects to chatter about during those hours.

During one of these sleepless nights, I suddenly became aware of a heavy weight lying across my legs. Then I felt a warmth penetrating the bedclothes, and heard a sort of purring. After that I became aware of a very distinctive smell, which I now know to be that of tigers.

At last I could see it: a gorgeous tiger lying across my lap. He was obviously very friendly. My husband had noticed I was distracted from our conversation and asked me what the matter was. When I told him he asked, 'Look at his head. Can you describe the markings?' I did, and my husband said that the 'he' was in fact a 'she' – Sabrina, a tiger cub that he and his family had brought up while they were abroad.

Charles's family were living in Egypt at the time, where his father was a government adviser. In the absence of properly trained veterinarians, Charles and his father treated many sick animals, including Sabrina. In time she became quite tame and domesticated, and was allowed to roam the grounds of their house at night as a means of protecting them. There was a certain amount of animosity towards the British at that time, and on one occasion a fanatic had fired at the family as they were riding along in a dog-cart. I hadn't known this until that night Sabrina's appearance spurred on my husband to tell the story. Apparently, a groom threw himself across my husband's sister, Georgina, as the bullets began to fly. She and Charles survived the attack, but unfortunately the heroic groom died. My husband bore scars from his bullet wounds for the rest of his life. Sabrina, therefore, was very important to his family, and no wonder my husband loved her.

After that, I saw her several times. If we were going out, leaving the house empty, she would appear as if to say 'Don't worry. I'm on guard.' But I did worry, because I wondered whether anyone trying to break in would *see* Sabrina. Her visits proved to me that if an animal has become individualized by prolonged contact with human beings, it can survive physical death the same as we do. Obviously, it was the bond of love between my husband and the tiger which had forged a link between them.

It is possible, of course, that any and every animal will survive physical death in this way, but spirits have told me that if you consider the pack nature of a herd of animals or a flock of birds, and the way they will all swerve simultaneously in one direction or suddenly wheel around in flight, you have the clue to the fact that they are all governed by a single, collective consciousness; share, as it were, one mind – and perhaps, too, one spirit. When one of the herd or flock dies, it is quite possible that it survives within the group awareness, even though the physical body is dead.

When animals, usually domestic, become individualized, displaying feelings and even thoughts, they have taken the first step towards developing an individual consciousness, which is probably why they survive as separate entities in the spirit world. Whichever way an animal survives, individually or collectively, it is perpetuated as surely as any human being. Animals are not a lower form of life – they may be a less evolved or different one, but they are still a wonderful manifestation of the same creative force.

My husband loved animals in this life, and he tells me that he has quite a zoo over on the other side now. He was always bringing home strays and injured birds and the like for us to look after, and I suspect that he is carrying on the good work even now, looking after pets until they can be reunited with their loved ones.

The question of killing and eating animals is a difficult one for me. Philosophically, I incline towards the Buddhist teaching on the sanctity of life in whatever form, though of course some life-forms like fleas or locusts are a nuisance or a threat, and so it is desirable that they should be got rid of as humanely as possible.

I don't much care for the fact that a living creature has had to die so that I can eat meat, but after discussions with doctors and dieticians alike I have been reassured that many people genuinely do need meat in order to remain fully healthy. And if animals were never killed for food, they would multiply dangerously, fall prey to natural disease or predators, and perhaps die in great suffering. After all, there are forms of life in the air we breathe, and in the water we drink. A vegetable is a living organism and may possess a sensory system. Vegetarianism is merely a question of where you choose to draw the line.

Only once has one of the spirit creatures I have seen really frightened me. It was a snake, and although it was in spirit form I was still quite scared. Animals and reptiles in the next world are not hostile to human beings, but, even knowing that, I was taken aback to see a snake rearing up before me. I described it to my husband, and once again it turned out to be an animal from his past. It was a hooded cobra that he and his father had found injured, and tended. They saved its life, and from then on it stayed with them.

Unfortunately, that wasn't the only snake I saw! Later on, after my husband had died, a second cousin would visit me frequently and on these occasions I kept seeing several different snakes together. What I didn't know at the time was that a boyfriend of my cousin's, who used to accompany her, used to work in a circus with a snake act. They all became his friends, he later told me, and he was very sad when, one by one, his friends passed on. He was pleased to hear they were back together on the other side where they seemed happy enough.

I know other people who have seen ghosts of pet animals so I'm not the only person in the world to have this experience. As I said in the last chapter, where there is love there is a link so it's not surprising that some pets come back to see their owners.

I've seen lots of pets, and some exotic animals like lions and tigers, but I think the strangest animal visit of all was a bear. I was staying with some friends in Switzerland, and the whole household was asleep except me. I tend to be a light sleeper and have got used to spending many an hour in the dead of night just lying in bed, thinking. That's just what I was doing when I heard a strange shuffling sound outside my door.

The shuffling gave way to snuffling, which went on for some time. Instinct told me it was some kind of animal, so I decided to investigate. I opened my bedroom door and there, standing before me, was a huge brown bear. It had a collar round its neck with a short chain hanging from it. It was very friendly, and seemed to me to be looking for a titbit to eat. I had nothing to give it, and anyway a ghost bear could hardly eat an earthly morsel. I remembered watching Barbara Woodhouse befriending large animals on television by blowing into their faces. So I just blew at the bear, hoping it would have a conciliatory effect.

It seemed to work, because the spirit creature just ambled away and disappeared.

I assumed that it had been a trained animal, perhaps from a circus, and that its owner had once lived or stayed in the house. When I got back to bed, I lay awake for a while and had to smile. I wondered if my hosts had heard me blowing through my mouth in such a peculiar way in the small hours of the night. If so, they must have wondered what had come over me!

Once, when I was visiting Christ Church priory, Hampshire, with my mother, I saw a beautiful white charger carrying a knight in shining armour. He was wearing the red cross of St George on a white tunic which he wore over his armour.

We were shown round the priory by an official guide, and he told our group of tourists that the priory was haunted by more than one ghost, and that at certain times of the day the ghost of a monk would appear. There were oohs and aahs from the tourists, and I was just about to speak and say I had just seen a knight on horseback when my mother nudged me in the ribs. I suppose she was right to shut me up. The rest of the people there would not only have thought me quite mad, they might have run away in terror from a 'haunting' that had actually taken place while they were there!

There are signs that animals can see ghosts, too. When I was a little girl, my family had two dogs. One was several years older than the other, and so died first. After the older dog, Toni, died, it was obvious that the younger one, Joy, saw her at times. She would be lying on a chair, peacefully snoozing, when suddenly she would open her eyes, gaze across the room towards an apparently empty space, then jump down and rush towards it. There she would stand, wagging her tail vigorously, presumably greeting her late canine companion. Who can say that Joy didn't see Toni? It seems unlikely that a dog would have hallucinations.

My present dog, Bella, seems very psychic. Sometimes she walks over to an empty armchair (I should say seemingly empty!), rests her chin on the seat and stays there for several minutes, wagging her tail and looking up towards an invisible person. I cannot always see who is sitting there myself, though I can feel a presence.

Sometimes I suspect it is my mother who has dropped in for a while. She was a great dog-lover and in fact tipped me off when the family who previously owned Bella were advertising in a local pet shop for a new home for her. I was just walking down the street one day when I saw my mother quite clearly. I had recently lost a much-loved dog and had decided not to buy another one. But my mother told me emphatically that there was a dog in need of a home advertised on the pet shop notice-board. I went inside, rang Bella's owners, and soon found myself with a friendly, exuberant canine companion.

It's hard enough trying to persuade people that you can communicate with spirits from the other side, without trying to persuade them that you can see birds and beasts too, so I usually keep quiet about the animals from the next world I have seen. I can guess what the cynics will be saying after reading this chapter: 'Oh, yes. Mrs Brown will be seeing pink elephants next!'

FAMILIAR FACES

In any account of the communication of psychics like myself with the spirit world, the names of well-known personalities will occur. Sceptics always seize on this phenomenon with glee. How come she only gets to meet the spirits of the famous? they wonder aloud, as if I and other mediums go in for some sort of psychic celebrity-hunt.

In fact, the truth of the matter is that I regularly encounter the spirits of people who were totally unknown in this life, except to their own relatives and friends. I am just as pleased and interested to communicate with them, and pass on messages to loved ones, as I am to talk to a famous composer or writer. But I am also privileged to receive visits from well-known people, in whose observations and messages a far wider section of the population will be interested. Sometimes, I have to admit to being surprised as to who actually visits me, and at the numbers who do. There are times when there is virtually a crowd of famous people all trying to give me a message – either to pass on to other people, or just messages of general hope for all of us. I try my best to give them all a fair hearing. Some of them, like George Bernard Shaw and Bertrand Russell, would talk all day and night if I let them.

In their life on earth these actors and actresses, musicians and composers, writers and public figures were in the business of communicating. It's not so surprising, therefore, that they are communicating still, and a sensitive like myself is a useful channel for conveying their thoughts and ideas back to a world which still remembers them with interest and affection. I hope, therefore, that I may be forgiven if in this chapter I concentrate on some of my more famous visitors.

Because I've worked almost exclusively with classical composers in the past, I was most surprised when John Lennon came to see me, comparatively recently, in spring 1985, and visited me quite regularly after that. I wondered at first why he had contacted me – I'd been aware of the Beatles, of course, but I can't say I was ever a fan. With two young children to bring up, I was too busy to follow the careers of a pop group. Nevertheless, that didn't seem to offend John. I look forward to his visits nowadays, enjoying his Liverpudlian chatter. I believe now he first visited me because he knew I was writing another book, and so took that opportunity of getting his most recent thoughts and work before the general public through me.

He is taller than I always imagined him in this life. I seem to see him as he looked at the height of the Beatles' early success – he looks to be in his late twenties or so, is clean-shaven, fresh-faced, doesn't wear glasses. I can feel great excitement and vitality emanating from him. He speaks quietly, tapping his fingers together but not his thumbs. His voice still bears a marked Liverpudlian accent, and when I commented on this once in surprise, he said, 'Oh, that's a part of me.' Liverpool went a long way towards shaping John's character, and he still hasn't lost his Liverpudlian traits.

I get the impression that behind the extrovert image was a deeply thoughtful character, a mystic really, though he often describes himself to me as 'just an ordinary bloke'. He says that had he been born into a different environment, he might well have become some sort of a philosopher, though he doesn't believe he would ever have become religious in the orthodox sense. He talks about the Maharishi frequently. Meeting him, John says, gave him a glimpse of the true meaning of life, though he was still rather baffled by life's enigmas, its hotch-potch of mixed values and beliefs. 'It takes you a long time to work it all out and very few people that I knew got very far in solving the mystery of life,' he told me once. 'I always thought we were not meant to know or understand everything during our life on earth. The trouble is, too many people have tightly closed minds.'

John told me he very much wants to give a message to the world; a message of hope and reassurance that there is ultimate peace, ultimate justice, a righting of all wrongs and a healing of all hurts. 'Ironically,' he explained, 'young people might be more ready to listen to me than to a religious leader. But what I have got to say is more or less what any religious leader says: that love is the only way, the only solution to life's conflicts and problems. The alternative path to love is destruction, self-destruction and world-destruction.'

In order to reach the maximum number of people with his messages, John has written a number of new songs and passed them on to me. I have put these into Appendix 2 of this book, and even as I write I am still receiving more new material of John's from the other side. But he's just as keen that his non-musical messages should get across, too.

John comes across to me as a rather reserved but very caring person. He says he never felt really satisfied when he was one of the Beatles, although they achieved great success. He always felt there was something more to life, and he was constantly searching, trying to find out what it was. He tried looking in all directions, and was still searching, right up to the day he died. Since he has passed over, he has been able to meet and talk to people who thought along the same lines as him, and were also always searching. Now, a lot of things are clearer in his mind, and he feels more contented as time goes by.

John's outer life didn't always correspond with his relatively developed inner life, so he had to cope with a certain amount of conflict within himself. He feels that this was reflected in his relationship with other people. He said – and this was obviously about the Beatles – 'The four of us were very individual. We worked well together musically, but we had our own separate ideas.' He said the four of them would talk into the small hours, but George was the quietest and didn't say as much as the others. When he did, though, it was often deep and profound – or, said John, blunt and to the point.

What has most surprised John is that there is a continuing process of learning and evolving on the other side. He told me that the 'after-life is very much a continuation of this life. You pick up where you left off. You don't suddenly change or know everything.' At first he found this puzzling, but now he is pleased that there are still new directions in which he may develop.

John has told me that sometimes he wishes he could recap on some of his past experiences, and even alter some of the things he has done. To use his own words, he says there were some things that, looking back, were 'Bloody stupid to do. But when you're young and trying to cope with life, you do silly things.'

During one visit, John told me that he had come specifically to ask me to tell young people: 'Don't mess around with drugs.' He can see now how much of a problem they are, and how much damage they can do. At one time, he thought some drugs weren't harmful, and even helped to soothe people, but now he realizes they are the thin end of the wedge, and he thinks it best not to touch any drug at all. John hopes that what he has to say on this matter might hold water with young people. At least they know that he has been there himself, been a part of the drug scene, and can look back and say: 'It was a big mistake to get mixed up with drugs. They bring you so easily to a point of no return, when no one can help you, and you can't help yourself.'

Sometimes, when John appears, he will do so in a great hurry, as if he has just thought of something and wants to pass it on to me before he forgets. While I'm hunting for pencil and paper, he will be chattering on at great speed. But you can't say to spirits: 'Oh, I'm busy. Come back later.' It may have taken a lot of effort on their part to get to you, and they won't always find you ready and prepared. That's why some of the things John has said to me, I can't recount in his exact words but have paraphrased from memory.

Looking at our world today, John thinks that the people of the West are living a too highly pressured lifestyle. Life has become too artificial for many people and our lives are geared too much to machines. People have lost touch with their roots, he says. He feels they would be much happier, calmer and healthier, if they would somehow connect themselves back to their roots. He feels that everyone needs to find some kind of philosophy, something that will have a steadying influence on them.

Sometimes he will change the subject abruptly – I think to give me a break from trying desperately to take down everything exactly as he says. And, to be frank, some of his thoughts are rather heavy-going.

I remember one thing he told me which made me laugh out loud, though he meant it in all seriousness. Still, he did manage a laugh himself afterwards, realizing that other people might find it amusing. He said he had always fancied himself as a gentleman, if not the titled sort. He wasn't being snobbish, he said; he just felt he might achieve a sort of dignity after passing through some very rough periods in his life.

Once, when I was talking to him, he thought back to how he was killed. When he was talking about the way he died, I started to pick up some physical sensations and felt as though I had been struck in the neck. John says he just remembers falling, and after that everything happened so quickly he didn't even realize he was dying. He told me categorically that he bears no malice against his murderer, Mark Chapman; he knows the man is mad. His feelings about his death centre mainly around his great pity for the suffering it caused so many people, particularly Yoko and Sean. He feels that, though his wife does have great inner strength, she was particularly vulnerable after his death. He feels very concerned for her still, almost paternally so.

He passed over so quickly that he felt afterwards as though many things had been left unresolved. At first, he found himself rather at a loss on the other side. He felt he still belonged primarily to our world, where he had always been a great partaker of new experiences. He felt isolated and cut off from this life but he soon realized that he could still observe events in this world, even if he could no longer take part.

He very often tells me that he is sorry to have broken various people's hearts in this life. 'But when you've got your own emotions pulling you in different directions, it's hard to find a solution that isn't going to hurt anybody. You get too uptight with the pressures and the travelling and you end up behaving in a way that isn't your real self.'

John constantly describes himself to me as 'just an ordinary person'. Despite all the adulation, he never felt he was all that special. He always felt it strange the way other people thought the Beatles were such a great group, because he believed that lots of other groups, given the same chances, would have been as successful.

Sometimes he feels guilty about the way the group manipulated their audiences, and once spoke for ten minutes on the way people allowed themselves to be manipulated today by political leaders, religious leaders, even the media. 'Life is about thinking for yourself,' he went on, 'working out your own destiny. What you do today is going to affect you – even as soon as tomorrow. You are building for the future, and for when the time comes for you to move on to the next life. A lot of people, when they arrive here, are sorry that they built for themselves such a horrible future because they have to work through that before they can move on to better things.'

John says that one of his greatest joys on the other side is to listen to people while they unburden themselves to him. He hopes people on this side will listen to his words and not think he is talking a lot of nonsense. Actually, John didn't use the word 'nonsense'. I changed it, while writing down his message, to what I thought was a more suitable word. John then appeared and said, 'What's in a word? I said "crap".' So, in John's own words, he hopes that people won't think he's talking a lot of crap. Sometimes he has others with him when he visits me, but I can never see them clearly enough to identify them, though I can tell that they are very close to John in spirit.

He asked me particularly to send his love to Cynthia, his first wife. 'I made a hash of that marriage. Sometimes I not only lost my heart but my head. Tell her I am deeply sorry. Give her my love. I still love her.'

John's eldest son, Julian, has followed him into the pop world, and John is pleased, if wary, about this because he knows what a tough, unsettled life it can be. But he still believes Julian will do well. 'Not because he's my son, but because he has really got talent, and I wish him well.' Also talking about his eldest son, he said, 'He's got a nicer disposition than I had.' He would very much like Julian to sing one or two of the new songs. 'I would be very pleased if he did,' he said to me. 'But tell him he doesn't have to if he doesn't want to. It's his life, and I wouldn't hold it against him if he doesn't want to.' I hope Julian does record a song or two of his father's. It would please John to know that through his son he's reaching a whole new generation of young people. But John doesn't want the public – or Julian himself – to feel that he is trying to use Julian to perpetuate his own image.

Another very important message which I have been asked to pass on concerns the fate of suicides in the next life. Those who believe in life after death often wonder what becomes of suicides, people who choose to propel themselves into the next world in an untimely way. From my conversations with spirit visitors, I have learned that the majority of people who commit suicide are not held responsible for this action on the other side. They are often literally out of their minds with pain or mental anguish. They are consequently not in control of themselves or their actions, and in these cases the stigma of self-murder is not held against them.

Very often suicides need to recuperate when they get to the next world. They are not always able to snap out of their misery or forget the terrible physical suffering they have endured before their death. But there are people in spirit who are trained to look after such souls, and close relatives and friends of the victim often help them, too.

Actor Alan Lake was one of those suicide cases who needed help to adjust and work his way through the deep feelings of remorse he felt as a result of his suicide. His wife, Diana Dors, was of course the great British character actress who died of cancer in May 1984. The following October, her distraught husband shot himself at their Berkshire home, on the anniversary of their first meeting.

I was surprised when Diana first called on me, but she struck me as a warm, vivacious personality, with a great sense of humour. She was brightly dressed in typical style – tight! – and decked out in her favourite type of jewellery – big and gaudy. She was wearing her hair loose and flowing around her shoulders, which she said was her favourite style because it made her feel younger. But she looked pretty young to me – in her twenties or so – plumpish, still, but very attractive. She talked very quickly and definitely, expressing herself fluently. I noticed that she faced me very directly all the time she was talking to me. I fancy that's how she must have been in this life, very open and direct.

Diana's main concern was Alan. She has visited me seven or eight times now, and wants to reassure everyone through me that he will be all right on the other side, despite the traumatic manner of his passing. She said she was looking after him in the new life into which he had so violently catapulted himself.

A few days after she first appeared to tell me about Alan, he himself accompanied her on a return visit, though he still looked harrowed and distressed by his recent experiences and didn't say anything at this point. He returned with Diana again, and managed to speak a little this time, then came on his own several times, when we talked quite freely. I felt great sympathy for him, remembering as I do the great anguish I felt when my own husband passed on into the next world. I know from my own experience that bereavement can be like a terrible illness, biting into you, but, unlike physical illness, there seems little you can do to relieve the agony. Time is, of course, the healer, but some people go beyond help before time can ease the pain. That was what happened to Alan. It would have gradually become easier for him to live without Diana, but his grief obliterated all his faith in happier tomorrows.

He speaks in a very distinctive way, with a pronounced sibilance on his 's' sounds that is not quite a lisp. Alan was quiet but quite as theatrical as he had been in this life. When he gave me the following statement on his suicide and its implications he was calm and appeared to be in full control of himself, though he seemed to have to take his courage in both hands to discuss this painful topic. I found what he had to say very moving, fully deserving of the care and attention with which he dictated his message.

> I see now that what I did was wrong and weak. I want to say that I'm sorry to all those who were so distressed by my action. I never was much good at facing realities, and Diana's death made me an emotional cripple. I ought to have stuck it out but I couldn't feel anything except a numbing grief . . . I

couldn't see anything straight. I couldn't take in what was happening to me. . . . It's such a relief to be able to talk about it and try to get things into focus. I want to try to make it up to all those that I gave so much trouble and sorrow. I'm sorry. Please forgive me. I'm ashamed now but I was too deeply buried in my own despair to be able to think what I was doing to others.

Diana is with me, helping me to make up for lost ground. She won't leave me, though she could move on to brighter planes. I have to work through my fears and sense of loss and come out of the darkness and despair that gripped me. I know now that when you love someone you can never lose them. But Diana seemed so utterly gone, disappeared for ever, that I think my mind gave out.

There's no one else like Diana, no one as special, no one so enveloping, as she was to me. When she went, I felt stripped naked, stripped of all that mattered in my world. Oh God, I remember the agony, the unremitting pain, the feeling of being locked up with torment, and with no escape. I couldn't stand it. I was drowning in my own sorrow, going down and down into a bottomless black pit. I was afraid of all those tomorrows without her; afraid of the loneliness; afraid of people looking at me and reading the agony in my face and seeing my suffering. Inwardly I was dying as well. It didn't seem to matter if I destroyed what was left of my life – it seemed so empty, so valueless, already nothing.

I'm not making any excuses for what I did, only telling how I pitched myself into eternity in a state of utter hopelessness. People should never lose hope, not even in the greatest sorrow. They should always hold on to that precious spark of light that glimmers on the horizon.

But I felt I was clutching at nothingness, with nothing to hold on to, to help me through the days ahead. Now I have to rebuild, to emerge from the deep abyss into which I sank. And I'm on my way up, thanks to kind helpers here, and to Diana.

Pray for me, and for Diana. And pray for yourselves as you face life's problems. Pray to be given strength. My thanks to all the people who had sympathy for me. That sympathy helps a lot, helps to heal the misery.

Remember me to my family, especially remember me to Jason, I let him down and I'm more than sorry.

I've seen Alan since that statement was made, and he's elaborated on his state of mind at the time of the suicide. He feels that one of his chief problems was that he bottled up his grief, was too embarrassed to let it out and share the depths of his despair with others. If he could have come out with all his feelings more openly, perhaps things might have been different.

But he's pleased to be able to pass on his thoughts about and experiences of suicide as he feels that people should view it in a more understanding and sympathetic light. It's not an act of will, in his experience. A suicide has all too often disintegrated emotionally; there is no steadying influence from within. A suicide is so full of conflicting emotions that one part of them, the destructive part, just takes over. Alan believes that this is not a legitimate cause for shame or condemnation, any more than terminal illness is. His only cause for shame is the way in which he left his son, Jason, to cope with the aftermath of his father's suicide. And the terrible shock and horror it caused when his body was found. 'I left Jason in the lurch,' he told me. 'And no father should do that. Human beings do terrible things to one another, but that's human nature. You just have to try to make things up afterwards.'

If he could have controlled things better, then for the sake of his son he would have. Alan feels that perhaps in his time on earth with Jason he was a little overwhelming in his attitude towards his son. He says that in many ways he didn't feel like a father to him at all, more like an elder brother. He's still got that feeling now, but he hopes to be able to exert a quiet, steadying influence over Jason from beyond. I know that Alan and Diana have revisited their luxurious home together in spirit. They said they were very happy there, and were looked after by a housekeeper who became more of a friend. They wanted to thank her for all her help and care of them.

I have seen Diana and Alan separately and together, and I'm not the only psychic who has. But its especially important to them to be seen to be together, as after Diana's death in particular there was a lot written about the couple in the newspapers. These articles made Alan very angry. 'People love muck-raking,' he said to me. He wishes very much that the memory of someone who has passed over could just be respected, but he would like to get on record his attitude towards the various romances Diana was reported to have had while married to him. He feels that if someone is of a warm and loving nature, as Diana is, it's very unlikely that they will love only one person throughout their lifetime. But so long as they do not deliberately harm anyone, there's nothing wrong in that, he adds.

After Alan's death, there was yet more written about them. One medium said categorically they could never be together again because of Alan's suicide. Eventually, Diana came to me, and in her usual businesslike, matter-of-fact way, she told me:

> I'd be grateful if you could dispel all the rumours that Alan and I are not together – I've heard that a mixed bunch of messages have been received from various mediums.
>
> Alan has been with me since the moment he died. Suicides arrive in the spirit life in much the same way as accident victims – that is, suddenly, without preparation, like someone bursting into a room unexpectedly. At least suicides know that they are about to die whereas accident victims have no such warning.
>
> Both suicides and accident victims need help to adjust to the sudden change. When people move house it often takes them a while to get used to their new home and to get to know their new neighbours. .

It's much the same with dying.

Supposing you are suddenly unrooted from your home and country and thrust into a foreign land? It would take time for you to get used to your new surroundings. But it helps a lot if, when you go to a foreign country, you know someone there who can show you around. It is the same with coming to spirit life. If someone meets you it can be a tremendous help, especially if you already know that person.

After Alan died I fought my way through his dark misery, through his feeling of total isolation, and made him aware of me by sheer concentration of love. Slowly, dimly at first, he began to be aware of my presence beside him and to feel my arms around him. I was crying because he had been through so much.

He began to see me and notice the tears running down my face and he forgot about himself in his concern for my distress. That is the turning point – when you begin to feel for others and not just for yourself. You reach out of yourself, out of your own sadness, to comfort someone else. You break free from your self-absorption, you begin to identify with others and you come out of your shell of self-pity.

God does not condemn anyone. It is only human beings that condemn one another. Sometimes the churches condemn suicides. God doesn't. God is pure compassion and complete forgiveness.

Alan was the victim of his own consuming grief. People can't help grieving, of course. It is a natural reaction. Why can't people care instead of criticizing? Do tell people who have lost friends or relatives through suicide that they are looked after and helped into the light.

While Diana told me this, Alan stayed by her side. He looked quite calm, and I knew that he would be all right. Diana was there to look after him, just as she had done in this life.

Another visitor I have been surprised yet delighted to see is that grand old Lancashire lass, Gracie Fields. I never met her during her lifetime, but I have seen her quite a few times since she passed on. Even though she lived in Capri for the last part of her life, she is still very much a lass from Lancashire, and her accent is as strong as ever.

One day Gracie told me that she would have loved to have been a dancer, but she thought herself too 'gangly'. She sometimes mentions Archie to whom, she says, she is still very attached. She also says it's wonderful to meet up again with your old friends when you pass on to the next life, but she has also discovered that one of the good things about the spirit world is that you can make new friends with people you might never have met on earth. Since passing on to the spirit world, Gracie has made friends with the famous coloratura singer, Galli-Curci, and has learned a few things from her about the use of her voice. 'Do you know,' said Gracie, 'although many people liked my singing, I learned from Madame Galli-Curci that I often misused my vocal chords!' Gracie said that Madame Galli-Curci has a tremendous personality: 'sunny-like, but she is very fussy about artistic standards'.

She told me she was always rather amused by her great success in this life. In her opinion, she was 'just another lassie with a bit of a voice'. But she thinks perhaps it was the sunny personality which resulted from her own happy, uninhibited childhood which enabled her to go out and speak to her audiences, making each one of them feel they were a personal friend.

Gracie has talked briefly about her childhood, and I always find it fascinating listening to her reminiscences about the old days in Lancashire. Gracie travelled the world and lived on the wonderful island of Capri, but her heart was evidently always in Lancashire. Talking about her early days, Gracie said:

> In the street where I lived there was no quarrelling. Everyone was matey. I think those childhood days taught me to be outgoing, taught me to share and to feel joy in life.
>
> It wasn't until I got here that I realized people sometimes have to be taught how to be happy. I

wish I could teach everybody all over the world to be happy. Happy people are kind people. It's only the miseries, the moaners, and the misers of the world who are cruel. I did my share of moaning at times, but my early days had taught me to always look on the bright side, to try to be cheerful, come what may. People nowadays don't seem to be very contented, yet they have far more than folks had in the old days.

Old Annie, who lived near us, had the least of us, but she was the one who always had a smile, and counted her meagre blessings as if they were in great abundance. She was a friend of my mum's, and used to help her out with the chores sometimes. 'Life's hard for you,' she used to say to my mother. 'It's easy for me. I only have myself to look after.' There was never a word of complaint from her about being lonely, but I think she must have been.

It's a funny thing. There's not nearly as much class distinction now, yet there are far more lonely folks. People don't mix as much as they used to. They are all sat in front of their tellies getting an eyeful of second-hand life.

Sometimes Gracie has sung to me and I've been spellbound by the loveliness of her voice, and honoured to have a private concert. She gave me the words and music of a song she has written since she arrived over the other side. The *Sunday Mirror* got to hear about this and they took the song up to Rochdale where it was performed by an old people's home. Gracie was thrilled to bits about that. The words of the song are given below.

MY SONG FOR THE WORLD

My song for the world – tra-la, la-la, la-la, la!
A song for the whole world to hear,
A song for the sad – tra-la, la-la, la-la, la!
To bring them a ray of good cheer.

When your heart feels like breaking,
And troubles come your way,
Remember that the night-time,
Is followed by the day,
So sing to the world – tra-la, la-la, la-la, la!
For the dawn cannot be far away.

My song for the world – tra-la, la-la, la-la, la!
To brighten that long, lonely road.
My song is for you – tra-la, la-la, la-la, la!
To lighten your life's heavy load.
When your dreams are all shattered,
And nothing seems worthwhile,
Remember tomorrow
May bring a happy smile.
So sing and look up – tra-la, la-la, la-la, la!
And your song will bring cheer to the world.

When I see Gracie now it is as an attractive young girl, wearing the clothes – even the old 'earphones' hairstyle – of her youth. She says sometimes, even now, it suits her to arrange her hair like that, and she told me that in her early days in this world she took great pride in her remarkably glossy hair.

Sometimes spirits appear to me and keep me guessing about their identity. One of these seemed vaguely familiar from newspaper photographs, but I still couldn't get his name. 'I'll give you a clue,' he said mischievously. 'I'm out on a limb – well, out on two limbs, actually – but it didn't stop me flying.' I guessed correctly then, much to his amusement, that he was Douglas Bader, the famous wartime pilot.

He was a bit hesitant over communicating, and a couple of times the line between us broke down. But he was determined to get over his message, because it was important to him, so I carefully wrote down everything he had to say:

Truth is bigger than bigotry. I never could stand bigots in my lifetime, and although I have now learnt to be more tolerant, I still have scant regard for those who see little beyond the end of their nose, simply because they won't look. Bigotry is sometimes like word blindness. People have a common habit of taking words at their face value instead of looking for the meaning behind them. People can often say one thing when they mean something else. Few of us can lay claim to a complete mastery of language and fewer still can lay claim to an ability to interpret other people's words.

A large number of people are limited in speech, and this applies to people who have passed into the world of spirit. People don't suddenly achieve command of verbal expression when they pass through the veil of death into life everlasting. As a result, many messages filtering through from the spirit world to the world temporal are not only poor in literary construction, but also poor in content.

I'm no orator, but what I have to say bears a straightforward message to everyone who is ready to listen to plain speaking from a plain-thinking man. I never could abide those devious types who twist sentences and make them so complicated that no one can understand them. So if I seem a bit blunt about some things, I hope I'm forgiven.

We fought a bloody war for freedom, for the freedom of all people, not just a chosen few. People are people, wherever they live, and whatever their skin colour, race or what-have-you. They all have the same basic needs, and they are all going to die one day. I don't mean all on the same day – I'd better add that, or people might think I'm forecasting a world cataclysm! When governments and all the other establishments which run the world get this clear in their priorities – the basic needs of people – perhaps there'll be more care devoted to these fundamental needs. But governments and other establishments often have their sights on other things, like trying to keep up with the other nations in the armament race. How appalling to think of all the vast sums of money being spent on the means to destroy life instead of preserving it.

I'm no statesman, no mouthpiece for weighty words of wisdom to impress the high-placed persons of the world, but I flatter myself that I could always confront a problem head-on, and sort it out or deal with it in a pretty direct and effective way. But governments often seem to shelve the urgent needs, the life-and-death needs of millions.

I don't want to dwell too long on the morbid side of things, so I'll talk about life over here. You don't need wings in this world. You can zoom about effortlessly once you've shed your ingrained ideas about gravity and the earthly limitations to movement. I think I was more surprised by this facility of volatility than anything else here. And what a boon to a chap like me who has been legless! No more of those wearisome twin contraptions that so often would not obey my will. Just a thought now will carry me in any direction that I wish to go. Here all your faculties are restored in full, and we grow in the image of our Creator as we are intended.

Douglas faded out here. It is often difficult for a line of communication to be held with the beyond, taking great concentration on the part of both transmitter and receiver.

Now let us turn to a legal gentleman who has quite often spoken to me from spirit. He introduced himself as 'Smith', which didn't tell me much! 'F. E. Smith, actually,' he elaborated, 'but call me "Fez".' I did not know anything about him then, and it was not until later that I discovered that he had been an eminent legal figure. Most of his communications were for a barrister friend of many years' acquaintance. His most recent utterance is for everybody:

Spirits are not always enlightening as to their whereabouts and activities. This, however, is not surprising, since many people are not very articulate. Their inability to communicate is further hampered by the difficulties to be surmounted when trying to establish contact with the world. Furthermore, it entails the business of trying to describe an environment that cannot really be appreciated until it is personally inspected. Try for yourself to describe a strange foreign country to someone who has never seen anything like it. You may find you have little success.

It is a known fact in legal circles that many witnesses in the witness box are unable to express themselves adequately or recall specific details, hence the need for expert attorneys to draw out the required information. I was regarded by many as a master of rhetoric; nevertheless, I find it by no means easy to impress my thoughts on the mind of an intermediary whose function it is to relay messages 'twixt heaven and earth'. In order to communicate with your world, I have to manipulate the fine, ethereal impulses which characterize some of our planes.

A high court judge once said to me: 'Smith, if we believed half of what we hear in court, we would be bumbling idiots, and hopeless judges of human nature.' Which observation leads me to remark that not enough emphasis is laid in schools and colleges on instilling a good command of one's native language. There would be fewer disputes and court cases if people knew how to say exactly what they mean to say.

Donald Tovey, the distinguished musicologist who died in the 1940s, heard that I was writing a sequel to my first book and gave me a lot of material for it. Since then there has been little from him, perhaps because I have been otherwise occupied. However, he has supplied the following message, and I am hoping that he might come through with some more messages before this book goes to the printers. If not, I think you will agree with me that in his case quality is better than quantity!

We have a lot of fun over here – good, clean fun. Our world is not a solemn, pompous place, though there are places set aside where souls can be quiet and meditate, or listen to elevating music. There are also dark places where those who wallowed in evil find themselves saturated in their own self-made misery. And there they stay until they turn in desperation to seek to improve their souls. Once they have admitted their wrongdoing, and truly wish to make amends, automatically a response comes to them from influences which will help them to climb out of the darkness. . . .

The spirit world is a world of endless opportunity, where those who wish to develop their talents can do so. The first few planes overlap the earth field of consciousness, and there is much interchange of ideas, although people on earth are usually unaware of this. . . . Your prayers for the dead can reach them and help them. *Their* prayers for you can reach you and help you if you are receptive to them. There is too much talk of 'here' and 'there' (your world and the hereafter) when in fact all life is one and interwoven.

The world of spirit is a more natural world than the earth world in a way. On earth, people are often forced by circumstances to live or work with other people who are uncongenial to them. Here, a natural law draws together those who are in harmony with one another.

I hope that these messages from beyond, from such a wide variety of familiar and famous names, will bring enlightenment and comfort to the readers of this book, for in every case the spirits who communicated them to me did so in a spirit of generosity and concern for those of us still in this life.

TWO GREAT THINKERS

Sometimes, receiving messages from people on the other side can be quite exhausting. However, over the years I've become used to working hard as I painstakingly take down whole new works from famous composers. But even so, I wasn't prepared for one of the visits I got a few years ago.

Without warning, George Bernard Shaw appeared. I wouldn't have recognized him immediately, I'm afraid. He was a bearded, youngish figure, who seemed to be in his mid-thirties or so, not the snowy-haired patriarch of the later photographs. He was dressed characteristically in plus-fours and a pair of sensible brogues. He identified himself in a crisp, efficient manner, told me he had something important to say about journalists – a warning to them – and I quickly grabbed a pen and paper to take down his opinions.

> Journalists, like many other species, are a mixed breed. Remember, what they write is for a living. That is to say they are likely to write from economic necessity what they think will earn them the most. There can be other factors which influence their writing – political leanings being high on the list, followed closely by religious persuasions. Add to those whatever personal bias a journalist may possess, and you have enumerated some of the hindrances to impartial reporting. I am not saying that reporting is, by and large, inaccurate, but I am

merely drawing attention to the reasons why reports may be diluted versions of the truth.

Had I been a journalist myself, which I was not in the real sense of the word, no doubt I, too, would have found myself writing jargon to please the public, or at least to please my editor.

Few people in the world can write or speak with complete honesty as this would prove devastating both to themselves and others. Where I am, however, we can speak truthfully, without risk to limb or livelihood. We, in our world, are not fearful for our reputations since these are established one way or the other, on our own worth of character which cannot be dissembled as on earth. In your world reputations are occasionally destroyed by false and malicious gossip. You live in a topsy-turvy world of inverted values where individuals are often set on pedestals on account of their wealth, rank or some other feature deemed to be desirable. Here we have nothing to commend us but our own qualities.

A warning might be advisable to those who think there is no life hereafter, and pay little attention to the state of their character. This *is* another life, I can assure them, and they will find themselves there eventually, minus the earthly props for their underdeveloped egos. A grim picture, you remark? Not at all. It is a picture of a just world, and what could be finer than that?

Well, that little outburst left me reeling! But it certainly gave me something to think about for the rest of the day. I took it down exactly as George Bernard Shaw told me to, and I must have proved to be satisfactorily efficient because a few days later GBS appeared again and told me he was going to give me a new play. In my previous volume of memoirs, *Immortals at My Elbow*, I gave an abridged version of a play, *Caesar's Revenge*; it had to be an abridged version because Shaw began to dictate it while I was in the middle of writing *Immortals at My Elbow* and I couldn't devote my whole time to him.

When the book appeared, Christopher Gilmore, a drama teacher living in North London, contacted me in great excitement. The play dealt with the theme of reincarnation – in a rather tongue-in-cheek fashion, in my opinion. But Mr Gilmore is a great Shaw fan as well as a member of an Eastern mystic sect, Eckankar, which propagates belief in reincarnation. He felt compelled to see that the play reached an audience and arranged a Fringe production of it at the Edinburgh Festival of 1978. I saw a performance, and thought he did a fine job.

Subsequently, GBS has begun another play. It took several sessions to get down the first scene of the first act. When it was finished, the playwright said he would be back with the rest, but for some reason he hasn't been. He might well appear at a later date, prepared to continue the play. In the meantime, here is the first scene of George Bernard Shaw's latest play, *The Heavenly Maze*.

Act 1. Scene 1.
An elegant drawing-room, reminiscent of the Victorian period, situated in the world beyond the gates of death. In one corner stands a superb grand piano at which is seated a pianist who is playing exquisite music. We cannot see who it is, for his back is towards us. The room is furnished elaborately and contains, among other items, a chaise-longue, on which the spirit of Isadora Duncan reclines gracefully. Nearby stands an immense armchair, in which is seated another spirit, that of the playwright himself. Isadora is dressed in flowing violet-coloured robes, and GBS is wearing tweeds. The pianist is dressed in a nineteenth-century-style suit.

ISADORA: I never knew that music could bring such intense pleasure.

GBS: Then you never really listened to it.

ISADORA: Nonsense. Of course I listened to

it. I had to dance to it.
Remember, dancing was my
métier on earth. It was I who
unfolded the art of the dance into
movements of subtle, sensuous
beauty hitherto undreamed of by
any dancer. It was I who
displayed what a marvellous
vehicle the human body could
become for the expression of sheer
emotion. It was I who—

GBS: (*hurriedly interrupting her*) Yes, yes.
We all know what a delightful
and delighting dancer you were.
And very grateful we are for all
you gave to the world.

ISADORA: That music! How it reverberates,
like ocean waves wildly
pounding, stirring my senses and
rousing my whole being. . . .

YANKEE   Yeah, kinda tears you apart,
VOICE: lady.

ISADORA: (*starting back in horror*) Who said
that?

GBS: It sounded like one of our modern
American cousins. (*Addressing the
voice*) Who might you be, dear sir?

YANKEE   Like you said, mister, I'm your
VOICE: genuine American cousin,
Patrick O'Toole.

GBS: Is that true now?

92

YANKEE VOICE:	Well, we both got Irish blood in our veins. I guess that does make us kinda distant cousins. Hi there, cousin!

(The owner of the voice appears. He is a dark-haired, blue-eyed man of medium height)

GBS:	The effrontery of the species never ceases to amaze me. Might I remind you, sir, that neither one of us has blood in our veins, nor even veins as far as I can tell, in our present bodies?
ISADORA:	Please don't mention blood, Bernard. You know how sick it makes me feel.
GBS:	I beg your pardon, my dear Isadora.
YANKEE:	Gee, you folks talk real pretty. I never heard no one talk that way in New York.
GBS:	So that is where you lived. How long since you left that God-forsaken city?
YANKEE:	God-forsaken! I know what you mean, mister, but let me tell *you* something. My folks weren't God-forsaken. They were Catholics.
GBS:	They might still have been God-forsaken in spite of that, or perhaps because of that.

YANKEE:	(*hotly indignant*) You gotta nerve, mister, saying that.
GBS:	No need to take it personally.
ISADORA:	Don't take too much notice of him, young man. He talks like that to everyone. It has become such a habit with him that he cannot stop it. He is quite a bore at times.
YANKEE:	Lady, now you're being rude about him. Don't nobody have any manners in this place?
GBS:	Manners, manners! What are manners but a cunning ruse to conceal one's true feelings? I believe in sincerity, sir, so I have no patience with the polite pretence of society.
YANKEE:	Ah, that clinches it.
GBS:	Clinches? Clinches what?
YANKEE:	They told me you are a guy for straight talking. No hedging around with him, they said.
GBS:	Who told you that?
YANKEE:	The two guys who met me when I bit the dust. They asked me was there anyone I wanted to meet? I told them that I had had a bellyful of double dealers, and wanted to see a guy who put all his cards on the table.

GBS: So you suffered at the hands of
                double dealers?

YANKEE: Sure did. That's why I'm here
                right now. They did me in, the
                dirty rats. And they were
                supposed to be my pals.

ISADORA: I do wish you would stop
                chattering, young man. I cannot
                hear the music because of your
                loud voice.

GBS: That is no way to welcome a
                newly arrived victim of murder,
                Isadora. The young fellow
                obviously needs to talk to
                someone. We will leave you to the
                music, and go for a walk. Come
                along, young man. I know where
                we can talk in peace.

                (*Exeunt GBS and Yankee*)

ISADORA: Thank goodness they have gone!
                Now I can steep myself in that
                glorious sound. Ah! I cannot
                contain myself any longer. I must
                dance. I must dance.

                (*She rises to her feet and begins to
                dance voluptuously*)

GBS told me on another occasion that he and Isadora had
been rather more than friends in this life. He certainly wasn't
known as a ladies' man, as far as I know, in the accepted sense of
the phrase, but he told me that he did in fact have a few very
good women friends – not necessarily platonic! When I
expressed surprise, he said that he had always kept a discreet

and gentlemanly silence on the subject. But 'You don't suppose I could write that way [about love] unless I really felt it!' he said to me once indignantly. And so I do believe he was writing from experience.

Although he never sent me any more of the play, the next time GBS communicated with me, he wanted to dictate a rather lengthy letter. When we are working together his characteristic stance is with his hands clasped behind his back, head inclined forward. He will take several jerky paces while dictating, then suddenly veer off in quite a different direction. When he has checked through my rendition of his words, he will nod his head decisively and say 'Good' in a very vehement voice. Here, in a slightly shortened version, is GBS's letter)

Dear Friends and Admirers,

A friend is not necessarily an admirer, nor is an admirer necessarily a friend. That is a simple enough statement, but it is calculated to give rise to some chagrin when, for instance, a particularly esteemed friend fails to shower one with the measure of admiration to which one feels entitled.

I discovered during the course of my long life on earth that my personal friends did not always or consistently like my work, and were sometimes the very last to applaud my efforts. This was very good for me because I laid far greater store by the opinions of my best friends than I did by the opinions of certain critics whom I sometimes suspected were jaundiced. Now I find the position somewhat changed. The observation that my essays and plays have well outlived me provides me with a source of comfortable satisfaction and mild amusement. To inherit such long-lasting veneration tempts me to conclude that posterity has grown more astute than I had hoped would be the case.

My admirers when I was on earth did not always brim over with friendly feelings towards me. However, now that I am safely out of the way, perhaps I am no longer to be regarded as such a formidable rival and therefore can be regarded in a more kindly light.

The dead do not seem to be such ready prey for the critics, who perhaps do not find it much fun to berate someone whose ears, as far as they know, are totally deaf to their remarks. Many people will more readily speak well of the dead than of the living, almost as if they are afraid that the dead might eavesdrop and rise up to haunt them, as I, indeed, am now rising up to haunt the unbelieving world.

Once dead, one might slide into oblivion as far as the world is concerned, one's life's work soon forgotten, one's existence remembered only by a few surviving friends and relatives.

The more fortunate find themselves held in continuing favour or taken up with greater fervour than when they were alive. I consider myself amongst the fortunate few who have had the best of both worlds. I own quite freely that I glory in my continued reputation, because it is good to be remembered.

We all have a basic need to be acknowledged as individuals, unless we have progressed to that state of assured inner self-hood in which one no longer feels that need of external reinforcements. Alas, many people pass on into the next life in a very indeterminate state, their individuality little more than a vague outline, their inner potential quite undeveloped. I have an economical turn of mind which makes me deplore wasted intelligence, whether it is wasted through failure to cultivate it or through misuse. I wish to stimulate mankind's intelligence into greater activity. It is a fact that the ultimate proof of man's immortality is not likely to transpire until the boundaries of science have been extended to incorporate the intangible and apparently inaccessible realms of metaphysics. Everything in the material realms originates in the metaphysical realms, and the realization of this profound truth provides the very foundation for the realization of man's immortality.

There are people who pursue the possibilities of communication with the disembodied out of idle curiosity, and others who hanker after it through a desire for personal messages. In my humble opinion, the most laudable motive for investigation into the possibility of communication is the desire to unfold the underdeveloped abilities of the human individual in order to understand them and put them into good service. The untapped psychic energies latent in human beings are in some ways greater than any powers yet discovered by the human race. These energies are beginning to manifest themselves in your midst and are as intrinsically divine as any other energy in creation. To harness these energies and put them to work for the benefit and evolution of mankind would rank as one of the greatest achievements of all time.

And this is a further communication I had from GBS in May 1985.

If I should talk to you from the Beyond where I am now, you probably wouldn't believe that it is I. So why should I bother? Well, there's always a hope that here and there people may wonder if it is myself indeed.

Oh, what fools we are when we're on earth to think that there's nothing more to come. I myself thought that there could be nothing more. I couldn't believe my good luck when I discovered myself to be still alive and in a body celestial, though perhaps not particularly celestial in my case. There was still too much earthliness in my soul, an earthliness I didn't want to part with at first. I was used to myself as I was, warts and all. I didn't fancy changing into an angel with a harp if that was what I was supposed to be. I didn't want to be one of the saved. Most of the people I knew on earth who said they were saved were, in my humble opinion, not worth the saving.

The people whose company I most enjoyed on earth were largely of the kind who would not have been on speaking terms with the Almighty. I often found saintly people boring, but the fault no doubt was mine.

I wondered why the Almighty had allowed an old renegade like myself to have a further existence after my departure from the world. It came to me little by little as I met others in this new life that there were plenty of people there who would not qualify for an extension of existence in the eyes of the Church. I wasn't in Hell, to be sure, but I wasn't surrounded by saints. It seems that God is more generous to souls like me than a good many preachers would be.

So here I am, preserved for posterity. The very thought might well strike terror into the hearts of my adversaries, and into the minds of all those self-appointed apostles of propriety and piety who disapprove of my good self. On the other hand, how reassuring I can be to the multitude of sinners who dread to think what may be in store for them in the Hereafter? The Almighty is not an ogre as some muddle-headed preachers would have you believe. He is not waiting to cast you down into fiery depths if your mind can't be made to accept some of the gobbledygook they prate; and if you are too honest to pretend that you accept such gobbledygook, you'll not be consigned to everlasting flames; they don't exist.

There are people in the world who want to browbeat you and frighten you into accepting their point of view, and to force you to agree with their beliefs. It seems that most of us have within us the makings of a dictator. We want to boss other people around, and we want to make them feel inferior. We want to make them feel that we are right and they are wrong. All these idiosyncrasies, when indulged, lead to conflict, war, and destruction. I really don't know when people are going to learn to live and let live: if they did learn that, most of the world's problems would disappear overnight. I doubt whether there'll be much left that you could call civilization in a few decades if people don't bury their various hatchets and just get on with living peaceably with their near neighbours and their far neighbours.

It's interesting to see how the bluff, no-nonsense Douglas Bader, the philosophical John Lennon and the literary genius GBS all pass on the same message about the advisability of abandoning the modern arms race if there is to be a real future for this world.

Another great thinker, with whom I often communicate, is Bertrand Russell. I must say that when he first introduced himself to me I was intimidated by his reputation as a great intellect. What could a brilliant man like that conceivably have in common with me? In fact, in my experience of him, Bertrand Russell is far from intimidating, except for the speed with which he fires off ideas and messages.

He speaks so quickly that I can barely keep up with him, but his voice is the clear, precise one of a lecturer, accustomed to conveying each syllable to a note-taking audience. His voice is rather croaky or raucous, but cultured and not very deep. He has a characteristic gesture of holding his chin in his hand, cupping his palm around the point of his chin with his thumb tucked beneath it and his fingers under his lower lip, except for his forefinger which extends upwards over the cheekbone. A friend of mine saw Bertrand Russell lecture in this life and remembers this characteristic pose very clearly. He also remembers hearing a couple of the opinions expressed by Russell to me, so perhaps they are favourite hobby-horses, though no less valid for that.

There's no hesitation when he speaks. His ideas seem to flow extraordinarily fluently, but he is always careful to present them to me in carefully thought-out terms so that we may feel on an equal level with him. Perhaps that sounds presumptuous but he has assured me that truly great ideas are always universal; anyone can understand them if they really try. The following statement by him should interest many people for its clear and cogent description of life on the other side:

> After breathing my last breath in my mortal body, I found myself in some sort of extension of existence that held no parallel, as far as I could estimate, in the material dimensions I had recently experienced. I observed that I was occupying a body predominantly bearing similarities to the physical one which I had vacated for ever: but this new body in which I now resided seemed virtually weightless and very volatile, and able to move in any direction with the minimum amount of effort. I began to think I was dreaming and would awake all too soon to that old world, of which I had become somewhat weary, to find myself imprisoned once more in that ageing form which encased a brain that had waxed weary also and did not want to think when I wanted to think.
>
> Now here I was, still the same I, with the capacities to think and observe sharpened to an incredible degree. I felt earth-life suddenly seemed very unreal, almost as though it had never happened. It took me quite a long time to understand this feeling until I realized at last that matter is certainly illusory although it does exist in actuality; the material world seemed now nothing more than a seething, changing, restless sea of indeterminable density and volume. How could I have thought that that was reality, and the last word of Creation to Mankind? Yet it is completely understandable that the state in which a man exists, however temporary, constitutes the passing

reality which is no longer reality when it is passed.

After my first contact with Bertrand Russell I pointed out to him (unnecessarily, no doubt) that if I did pass on what he said, there was no guarantee that it would be accepted as a bona fide message from him. This was his reply:

> My influence on the thinking of the masses was negligible, but a strange quirk in human nature leads some people to pay more attention to messages from supposedly discarnate beings than to any from the mouths and pens of mortals. Therefore I am hopeful of my disembodied utterances being at least a source of diversion amongst those who foster an attitude of greater respect for the dead than the living.

When he said this, I suspected he was having a sly dig at the type of person who hangs open-mouthed on every word emanating from the next world as if it is a tremendous revelation from on high. Not that I exclude the possibility of great revelations from the beyond, but I know well – as Douglas Bader remarked in the last chapter – that a large quantity of banalities emerges from contact with the average after-death communicant. At the same time, we have to remember that these very banalities are the meat-and-drink of our everyday social talk, and I do not see why we should be surprised when those who have passed on continue to indulge in this habitual practice.

Suppose you knew a man who lived in the next road, and his main interests in life were a football match and a glass of beer. If he died, and had a shot at communicating with you after his death, would you expect him to pour out a stream of pious eloquence? Would you not be tempted to doubt his identity if he did? People can only prove their identity by being themselves, and acting and speaking in a recognizable way. 'A superficial examination of the facts rarely reveals the truth. There are those whose summary consideration of a controversial matter dismisses their opinion as shallow and immature,' Bertrand

Russell commented on another occasion. He then explained in more simple terms that he could appreciate now, from his greatly increased perception into people's minds, that the majority of us do not give a really considered opinion on many issues.

> I did not realise [he added], just how many people there are who are unwilling to consider all possibilities with regard to the hypothetical aspects of religion. There are so many possibilities which they want to exclude without giving them any thought, or allowing others to give them any thought. We are no longer in the Middle Ages when a man could not question the existence of God or anything about Him except on pain of death. We must let it dawn on us that if God exists and is a reasonable being He would prefer an honest doubter any time to a credulous cretin.

I thought the expression 'credulous cretin' was a little too sweeping, and said so. For the first time in his talks with me, he showed some irritation. 'If you are going to take it on yourself to edit my speech,' he remonstrated, 'I shall say even more outrageous things and insist you do not expurgate them.' I was a little amused, since I felt I held the whip-hand and could choose to omit any portion of his remarks I liked. He continued:

> The assessment of any man's value rests not only upon the sound judgement of those who sit in judgement but also upon a profound penetration into the hidden attributes and tortuous labyrinths of his mental processes. No human being is as simple in psychological function as might have been construed a century or two ago. There is rarely a straightforward assumption which can rightfully be relied upon to state a man's composite attitude; motive is almost invariably mixed with sundry and subtle undercurrents in the individual's own interests which would build a cynical view if

one did not regard the main motive as the true indication of character.

The human mind works very much upon the principle of computerization if it is endowed with healthy intelligence and primed with adequate knowledge; it will weigh up all aspects programmed for its prognostication, therefore taking in its stride both the altruistic and self-seeking venues. The final decision is often arrived at prematurely before the inbuilt computer of the mind has been allowed to assimilate all the known facts and to complete assessment. Complete and effective programming is the secret of efficient mental activity; and how often can we be certain that our programming is absolute and accurate, unbiased by false propaganda from the outer world and distorting influences from within ourselves?

He speaks in this passage as if still in our world, still taking a close interest in the evolution of the human mind. In another conversation with me, it seemed apparent that he had altered some of his conclusions since his transition into spirit.

The scientist cannot be reproached if his study and research have sometimes drawn him to wrong conclusions which later discoveries have caused him to recant.

An examination of the process of evolutionary thought will reveal that it has a directional impetus very like a watch-spring which has been released from its tension and widens its concentric rings, becoming free from being geared to time. The primitive brain can deal only with the present moment of time; a brain more sophisticated can review the past and preview the future. Even in the world of matter it is possible to transcend time in thought, also in actual fact to a distinctive degree by fast travel removing one from parochial time. Time and location are inextricably interwoven to such an extent that one begins to conceive that time is a place rather than a process.

On another occasion, he delivered the following speech.

Shedding light on humanity's path is not going to be an easy task, whoever attempts it. Ideas and ideologies can only be introduced slowly, and the means of doing this is still limited to personal conveyance among millions who remain to this day semi-illiterate or totally so.

Throughout the world, many a person convinces himself if not others that his line of thinking is superior to theirs and best for the populace in general. The acid test of priming the populace is in the test-tube of the experience which follows for those subjected to the priming process. Is their experience the richer materially or mentally, and are they healthier or happier through having had certain ideas moulded into their minds? Are they living more constructive and co-operative lives as a result of having submitted what intelligence they may possess to the manipulations of others?

It seems difficult for nations to adopt a system of government which is satisfactory to the whole populace, and there must always be the dissenters who cannot agree with the policies practised by the current leader or leaders. By some strange freak of outlook, almost all dissenters are regarded as seditious influences – as indeed they may prove to be in many instances; but the remnant who cannot be so classed may consist of genuine well-doers whose aims are solely to introduce reforms that will rectify various evils both social and economic.

And on another occasion I received the following related thoughts:

Each of us should choose his or her own path.

Millions never have any real choice because they are conditioned from birth to accept certain fixed beliefs. If, later in life, they are able to examine those beliefs objectively, and come to accept them, then those beliefs may become a genuine individual view, instead of merely being superimposed. Beliefs with which we have been indoctrinated before our powers of reasoning developed are regarded by me as being invalid. They are not an intrinsic part of us. They are somebody else's beliefs, not our own.

Habit dies hard. If you are habitually bombarded with certain thinking patterns you are very likely to absorb them. If you are habitually subjected to certain advertising techniques, you may well be coerced into accepting their mesmeric effect. Propaganda, continually pumped out, may overcome people's resistance to it if it is sufficiently forceful and persistent.

It takes courage to break away from the herd, courage to risk the disapproval of the herd, to stand alone for what we believe is true. If the Christian martyrs had not stood their ground, Christianity might have perished soon after its inspirer. If the suffragettes had not prevailed, equality for women, who for so long have been downgraded and oppressed, might never have been put in motion. If medical pioneers had not braved ridicule, many medical advances might never have taken place. The very people we decry today, we may applaud tomorrow.

On another occasion, he posed the question:

Is happiness for all Mankind an impossible ideal? Perhaps it is, but that should not deter us from cultivating it as widely as we can. To begin with, we must allow for the contingency that human nature is not always arable, just as the soil is not always arable, to stretch the metaphor a little. Land can often be made arable, or more arable than it was. Human nature, too, can be treated to make it more fertile by feeding the imagination, by implanting good silage to enrich the foundation before hopefully sowing seeds that will bring forth a good harvest in the person of a happy member of society who will in turn give happiness to other members of society.

A great amount of time and energy has been spent in the pursuit of happiness by a great many people since time began. Given the fundamental prerequisites of bodily health and well-being, happiness would seem reasonably easy to obtain, so some might presume. But we know, from the high number of depressed individuals and the increasing percentage of suicides, that this is plainly a fallacy. What is it, then, that will assure happiness for us, all obvious causes of discomfort and pain having been ruled out?

There can be no universal panacea for happiness which is obvious to anyone who has studied, as I have, the root cause of happiness and its opposite. Happiness is a state which is created within us by a very large and very varied number of factors. One man is happy with nothing less than a luxurious mansion and estate and a fleet of fast cars; another man is happy in a monk's cell with the minimum requirements of life. It would seem, therefore, that it is not what we actually possess which provides us with happiness, but our reactions to what we possess. The secret of happiness, like the kingdom of heaven, must be within us, and the key to it is our attitude towards life, especially towards our own personal life.

Can we teach people to be happy in the same way as we can teach them to add, subtract, multiply and divide? To do that, we would need to teach them to read their own selves just as we teach them to read literature. This would mean beginning with the alphabet of self-analysis which could not easily be taught to children since standards of comparative behaviour need to be studied before self-analysis can effectively be undertaken.

Happiness is to a large extent dependent on our disposition. We say that someone has a happy nature and that someone else is nothing but a miserable worm. We need to discover how to bestow a happy disposition on people and at what age this can best be achieved. Childhood would seem the period of life in which to create a happy disposition because in most individuals the disposition developed in childhood remains with them throughout the rest of their life. The question is whether children in general possess an intrinsically happy disposition, which certainly seems to apply in the case of healthy children. If, then, they appear to be born with a happy disposition, it would seem a natural tendency, a tendency which oftimes becomes despoiled as they grow up.

If happiness is the natural tendency, all we need to do is to discover how to retain this tendency, or to avoid having it impeded or destroyed. This brings us to the question of environment and upbringing, education and general experience, a galaxy of considerations which cannot adequately be covered in this essay.

Some environments are certainly not conducive to health, and therefore not conducive to happiness. The same applies to upbringing, and extends also to the matter of education which aims to inculcate knowledge without concerning itself with anything as unintellectual as the pursuit of happiness. General experience is something over which we do not have much control, and we have to take what we get and make the best of it. The attitude of an individual can enable him to rise above general and personal tragedies and still find happiness in living, demonstrating that experience, in whatever form it comes, need not deprive us of our total serenity. Our reactions and our attitudes, the former being largely dictated by the latter, are key factors in our search for happiness. It therefore appears that the influences which determine our attitudes are of paramount importance. We have to admit that our attitudes for the most part are determined for us by others, at least until we reach an age when we can reason and think for ourselves.

Health, which might be termed bodily happiness, depends on a varied and adequate diet, a healthy environment, and sufficient exercise and rest. The health of the mind, which one would take to be synonymous with mental happiness, must depend on similar conditions. The mind needs variety to avoid boredom which is one of the main causes of unhappiness, and it certainly needs a mental climate which is propitious to its well-being. It also needs to be exercised to keep it in good form so that its interest in life can remain keen and ward off the onslaught of boredom. Rest for the mind is probably one of the most essential requisites for its happiness, for tiredness and zest cannot go hand in hand, and happiness calls for zest.

And recently Bertrand Russell has contacted me with more words of wisdom. Some people, I know, find him rather heavy going – can you imagine what it is like for me to take all this down? – but I know he has many devotees who will be interested to know his latest thoughts. Here is his latest communication:

Had we been made perfect, in the first place, it might be argued that we could not go wrong.

Mankind is the product of aeons of time, having evolved from an idea in the Eternal Mind. If we believe that the Eternal Mind conceived us, we cannot help but accept the inference that it is responsible for our nature. Only if we had made ourselves could we be held responsible for our state.

If a potter misshapes some clay, it is futile for him to blame the clay for its malformation. I am suggesting to you that mankind may not be as responsible for its misdeeds as has been supposed. People talk of free will, of the choice between good and evil. A perfect being would exercise its free will with circumspection, and always make a correct choice.

I am not in any way suggesting that people should not be held responsible for their actions. Responsibility, like any other faculty, is an evolving quality. We recognize this fact when we excuse children from being entirely responsible for offences which they may have committed.

There's a good deal of food for thought in these opinions but, if you'll excuse my saying so, there are times when I could wish that Bertrand Russell didn't have so many!

However, with the next General Election looming into view, the following observations seem to be quite topical. They were actually dictated to me by Bertrand Russell on 26 April 1979.

Whichever party is voted into power by the electorate, it should be borne in mind that the successes and failures of every government are contributed to by the actions of the populace. There is an attitude, on the part of some voters, of non-participation in the nation's affairs once they have cast their votes. It is as if they abandon all sense of responsibility for the nation's progress thereafter in the belief that it is the ruling party's responsibility alone. This is the cause of many industrial and social troubles. No government can govern successfully without the co-operation of the people. Recent events have indeed demonstrated this to be the case.

If the people of this nation truly desire that the country should be conducted into a stable and expanding prosperity, they should realize that this can only be achieved by the combined efforts of all its members, and not merely by the efforts of its parliamentary members.

Political parties all have their strengths and their weaknesses. There is less divergence in their principles than there was in my time as a young man. There is, however, still a great deal of confusion in the minds of many people regarding the policies which the various parties represent.

It is to my profound regret that I observe a considerable amount of class prejudice still being fermented and perpetuated. It is, of course, foolish to the point of disaster to stir up strife between people, between races, or between sections of the community. You must seek out ways to resolve your differences by peaceful means, for the more aggression there is, the more bitterness is fostered, and the greater number of people who suffer as a result.

In the struggle for survival, there are people who do not care whether they increase the burdens of others or hasten the nation's downfall. This downfall ultimately becomes their own downfall, a penalty which they seem to overlook. If they do not want to undermine their own interests as well as the nation's as a whole, they must behave in a manner befittingly democratic, working for the general good, and not simply for their own good without due regard for the welfare of others.

This is my recommendation on the eve of the election:

Don't just vote –
Pull your weight.

THE COURAGE OF VIKTOR ULLMANN

I did not know Viktor Ullmann in this world. There was little likelihood of our meeting as he lived in Czechoslovakia and I have lived all my life inside a few square miles of South London. During the war years I was working in a clerical capacity as a civil servant, and also taking part in the government-organized Mass Observation programme, which monitored civilian morale and lifestyles throughout the war years. I was, of course, aware of the huge influx of refugees at that time, from Central and Eastern Europe, but, in common with most other people, I had no idea at all of the scale of the atrocities being practised in Hitler's concentration camps.

I first met Viktor Ullmann more than 30 years after he was murdered in the notorious Auschwitz camp, when I was privileged to help him revise an opera he wrote in Theresien-stadt under appalling circumstances. Our meeting took place in a rather roundabout way. In 1976, the very distinguished young pianist, Howard Shelley, was recording some of the music that I have received from the composers. The recording session was taking place in the famous Abbey Road Studios in North London, and Howard had asked a gifted conductor, Kerry Woodward, then Director of the Netherlands Chamber Choir, to assist with the editing of the tapes of his performance.

I had never met Kerry before, but he said he had heard of my work and would love to have the opportunity to talk to me further about it. Obviously, there was no time then – studio time is very expensive indeed – so it was arranged that he would visit me at home where we could talk at length. We had no idea that when we did eventually meet to talk about my work, and parapsychology in general, we would be joined by the spirit of Viktor Ullmann.

However, as Kerry and I were talking, I became aware of the spirit of a man, standing in one corner of the room, with Liszt beside him. I described this spirit to Kerry – he had very close-cropped hair and deep-set eyes – and then I asked the spirit's name. He answered that he was Viktor Ullmann. I thought it was a German-sounding name but Liszt intervened to announce that my visitor was 'of Slav descent'. Viktor was speaking German, which was not a language I was familiar with at that time, so Liszt acted as translator.

Viktor began to talk about an opera he had written while in a concentration camp, Theresienstadt, in Czechoslovakia. The short, complete opera was called *Der Kaiser von Atlantis* (*The Emperor of Atlantis*). Viktor said that some of the guards had been kindly disposed to him and had smuggled in bits of paper for him to write his opera on. The score was later smuggled out of the camp and eventually reached London, where it came into the possession of an old friend of Viktor's, a Dr Adler. All this was totally unknown to me, and there was no chance of my ever having seen the score, which was, and still is, unpublished.

On the very day he visited me for the first time, also quite unknown to me, Kerry had the original – and only copy – of the score with him in his briefcase. Kerry had happened to meet Dr Adler, who told him about the opera he had had in his possession since the war. Not unnaturally, Kerry was very interested in a score written in such circumstances and asked whether Dr Adler would let him see it. Once he had examined it, he felt that something should be done with such a remarkable and historic work.

Kerry knew the story behind the opera, but I heard it first from Viktor Ullmann himself. He told me that when the opera was complete, he organized a performance of it in the camp with the help of other prisoners who could sing or play. Der Kaiser himself, who represented Death, was a rather thinly disguised caricature of Hitler, and the message of the opera was that you cannot destroy the spirit of a race.

Some of the German guards realized the political message behind the opera and this, no doubt, was one of the reasons why Viktor and his young librettist, Peter Kien, were transferred to Auschwitz, a very much tougher camp, where they eventually perished at the hands of the Nazis.

Viktor began to talk in great detail about the score, naming exact page and bar numbers, and quoting what was written in each instance. He asked for a number of amendments and additions to be inserted in the score. Kerry noted what Viktor said and made the alterations where indicated. All this was done without my even seeing the score for myself!

Viktor thanked Kerry for his interest in the opera and all he had done to try to get it performed. Then he asked him to turn to page 11. Here was a recitative with harpsichord accompaniment. Viktor wanted this adapted for flute, violin and cello. He then asked Kerry to make a section on page 21 the same as on page 11. Then Viktor said, 'Turn to page 46, to the viola part.' The rhythm here was a half-note followed by a quarter-note. He wanted this reversed. Kerry had felt it was incorrect as written, but the amendment sounded correct.

There were two other sections which Viktor wanted fully orchestrated. The aria of 'Death' in the middle section had been scored for harpsichord only. Viktor wanted it written out for the flute, muted trumpets, muted strings and a bell played rather freely.

I could not even see the score from where I was sitting, and it was the only copy in the world, yet Kerry had no difficulty at all in following my detailed comments, which all checked out exactly with the manuscript before him. What struck me about all this was that the composer of the opera, Viktor Ullmann, obviously had complete recall of every note on every page of the opera. Perhaps, written in such terrible conditions, it was engraved on his mind to the last detail. Or had he perhaps a means of referring to or reading the score, or an etheric double of it?

Kerry went away and worked for two weeks on the score, carrying out Viktor's requests for amendments. Kerry freely admits he is not a composer, though he does, of course, understand scores. But, as Viktor had predicted he would, he felt inspired in carrying out his work on the score, and thought that the inspiration he felt must have come from Viktor himself who had told me he would help with the orchestration of certain parts.

After these two weeks, Kerry came to see me again. Viktor then appeared in spirit and told Kerry that he had done very well. But he added, with Liszt translating, that he wanted the flute and muted trumpet parts reversed. Also, he said that Kerry had put the funeral bell on the wrong note. Kerry had in fact written it for the note B flat and Viktor asked him to alter it to half a tone lower. This simple alteration, Kerry said, completely transformed the sound and effect, making it much more mournful and dramatic. I had not known what he had written for the bell, and of course I had not heard the opera. By now, Kerry was utterly convinced that I was communicating with the mind of Viktor Ullmann.

Eventually, the opera was shown on BBC television, complete with all the amendments and additions supplied by Viktor Ullmann himself after his death. It has been produced since, always to rave reviews, and my own rôle in its revival was the subject of several newspaper features which reached as far as the United States.

Viktor also spoke to me about the conditions in the camp where he died, and referred to the dreadful and unmistakable stench there. In fact, he somehow conveyed the idea of the pervading stench to me so strongly that I could actually smell it. It was something I shall never forget; I can only describe it as a sickening, rotting smell. Once Kerry made as if to hand the opera score to me, and I put out my hand to take it, but something made me recoil in horror. Suddenly, the thought of handling that score brought back the stench so vividly that I just couldn't touch it.

Viktor also related how he died, together with many others, in a windowless shed, sealed up from the outside, into which a poisonous gas was infiltrated through an inlet in the roof. Viktor said the prisoners had been stripped of their clothes, and told they were to go into the shed for de-lousing treatment. In the midst of the terrible darkness, the victims gradually realized that they were being exterminated. First, said Viktor, a strange violent chill swept over them, and then they began to shake and cough and stifle. Liszt translated: 'They could have shot us instead. It would have been quicker, but perhaps they didn't want all that mess.'

The Nazis had destroyed the bodies of the Jews, but they couldn't destroy their souls. Here was one of the victims, proving it! He was a man of outstanding courage who cocked a snook at Hitler – and a snook which has long outlived its target. Certainly, my encounter with Viktor Ullmann has been one of the most dramatic psychic experiences I have ever had, and I wish his opera could be heard more widely as an example of supreme triumph over bitter adversity.

FORESEEING THE FUTURE

Idon't usually try to see into the future because I feel that we are living in the present and should try to concentrate all our attention on what is happening now. But I do have occasional glimpses into the future, sometimes when I am conscious and sometimes when I am asleep, through a dream.

We have a family joke that Mum can read the tea-leaves. It's all a bit silly really because I've never gone in for that sort of fortune-telling but we have discovered that I do seem to be able to read them. In fact, I think my seeing into the future is just a matter of concentrating very hard on one point; traditionally that point has always been the leaves in a cup, but it could just as easily be the back of the cornflakes packet, or even some inner point if I concentrate with my eyes shut. If I just concentrate very hard on one fixed point and let my mind go clear, I can occasionally receive impressions of the future. I don't 'see' it in the sense of a visual image, necessarily: I just become aware that a particular thing will happen.

For instance, on one occasion my son, Thomas, who works for a bank with international connections, was detailed to go on a business trip with a colleague. They were to visit several places, carrying out negotiations for their bank, and planned to travel by ferry and car. Thomas had never driven on the Continent before and was a little apprehensive so he asked me, half jokingly, to read his tea-leaves on the subject. I solemnly looked into his cup and told him the trip was going to be pretty routine, rather boring in fact. Then I told him he would return a day ahead of schedule. 'That's impossible,' he said. 'The ferries are already fully booked. We had quite a job to get our return booking. You must be wrong this time.' But it all looked pretty clear to me.

Thomas and his colleague went off on their trip and, unbeknown to me, finished their business a day early. They managed to get a last-minute cancellation on a ferry and Thomas turned up at home a day earlier than planned! Naturally, I was delighted to see him, and even more glad that the tea-leaves had been vindicated.

Anybody with this sort of gift has to be very careful when applying it. You have to be constantly on your guard not to let your subconscious or wishful thinking lead you astray. I think I find the process made easier by my early training in Yogic Meditation which taught me to concentrate profoundly on the one image instead of being distracted by other things.

Einstein once gave me an insight into the way I seem to be able to see into the future by telling me 'Time is a continuum.' He says that time is not separated into independent sections, but flows in a curving form. Therefore, those with the mastery of time, if they look in the right way, should be able to see ahead or behind them on the curve. He gave me the following analogy to explain the structure of time further.

Imagine you are travelling on a train which is going round on a bend in the track. On looking out of the window to the front, the future can be seen ahead; and looking towards the back, the past is visible. It's a simplified explanation, of course, but it gave me a rough idea of how foresight and hindsight can occur.

Besides seeing into the future, I am sometimes given a different sort of insight when I receive a spirit message about a future event. A few years ago, a good friend of mine, Vicki Mackenzie, was about to jet off to Hong Kong to start a new life. She had given up her job on a Fleet Street newspaper, sold her flat and was all set to go when I got a prediction from beyond conveyed by Liszt. He told me that Vicki would be unhappy in her new life; she would realize almost as soon as she set foot in Hong Kong that she had made a mistake but her pride might prevent her from admitting it. I was asked to tell Vicki this, and to say she should come home whenever she felt like it, not worrying what other people might think.

She told me later that she felt worried and rather cross that I should say this just days before she was due to depart. And when she was in Hong Kong, and very unhappy, she refused to leave because she was so determined not to be influenced by my words of warning. But then, wrote Vicki, 'Common sense prevailed, and within a week I'd packed up my job, my flat, and was on a plane back to England. The instantaneous relief and joy I felt was ample evidence that I'd done the right thing. Hong Kong wasn't for me and Rosemary's message was absolutely right.'

The message from the other side didn't go into any detail as to why Hong Kong wouldn't work out, and in fact Vicki herself couldn't pinpoint exactly what went wrong. Her attempts to start a new life just didn't feel right, she said. Obviously, someone on the other side knew how it would all turn out and was aware, more than anything, that Vicki would feel a bit of a fool coming home. I like to think that it was because of Liszt's advice that Vicki was able to find the courage to come back and take up where she left off.

The story has a happy ending, too. She bumped into an old friend who sold her his flat at a bargain price; she quickly found work; and, more important than anything, she found peace and the settled life which had eluded her in Hong Kong. Someone, somewhere, was looking after her!

Such prophetic messages aren't terribly common though. Most spirits feel that it's no kindness to throw a shadow over someone's mind by telling them of something bad to come, unless the harm is something that can be averted. Besides foreseeing the future, other insights – the majority, in fact – come to me in dreams. If I wasn't used to my dreams coming true, it could be a bit unnerving. Even so, sometimes little things happen that make me do a double-take.

There was an occasion when I was going to the Festival Hall to a concert with my son and one or two friends. The night before, I dreamt that we had reached Waterloo Station, got off the train, and were walking through to the Festival Hall. In my dreams, I saw us passing an old tramp. I saw his face, his features, and his expression. I saw his clothes, his hat and the colour of his old coat. He made a very vivid impression. It was a funny thing to dream about but when I woke up I just dismissed it as one of those strange things the subconscious mind throws up from various events in the past. However, when the next evening came, we got off the train at Waterloo, started to walk through to the Festival Hall, and there was the tramp leaning against a wall – exactly as I had seen him in my dream. I was a little startled and then I thought perhaps there was a reason why I had dreamt of him. The only thing I could think of was that perhaps he needed help. I certainly wasn't in any position to alter his financial situation greatly, and instinctively felt that it wasn't help of that sort that was required. I felt the best way I could help was to say a prayer on his behalf, asking God to help him.

I always try to analyse the things that happen to me, the ordinary everyday things and the psychic things, to see what constructive use they can be put to and to try to decide whether they are guidelines for me to follow in a certain way. I dreamt once that I had weighed myself and found I weighed 11 stone. I had been ill and was under instructions from the hospital to build myself up with lots of liver and a bottle of Guinness every day. I know Guinness is fattening, and I must have been a little afraid of what it was doing to my weight. When I got up the next morning, I said to my daughter, 'I dreamt I weighed eleven stone.' She burst out laughing and said, 'There's no way you could weigh eleven stone.' We were still laughing when we went to the bathroom and I stood on the scales. We were both absolutely horrified when the needle stopped dead on the 11-stone mark! I gathered that a friendly spirit from the other side was giving me a nudge, saying 'Watch it. You don't want to get too heavy.' Anyway I began to diet that very same day.

Another, earlier, instance of a dream coming true, was more like a nightmare. When my husband was still alive, we were very poor because he had been unable to work owing to ill health and, as a self-employed man, there was no unemployment benefit for him. When Georgina was born we needed a cot for her and the only way we could get one was on hire purchase. Because of our circumstances, we fell behind with the payments. During this time I had a terrifying dream. I dreamt there was a knock at the front door. I went to open it, and standing there was a little man with a really horrible face. He said he had come to take something back. . . . In the dream he didn't say what. Then, some days later, there was a knock on the door, I opened it, and the same little man with the horrible face said he had come from the hire purchase company to reclaim my baby daughter's cot. He took it, and even though my husband and I were sad and shaken we were able to take comfort from the fact that I had been forewarned.

I know a lot of people who get warnings or messages or glimpses into the future in their dreams. Our previous vicar and his wife used to dream lots of things before they actually happened, and would talk about it quite freely. I think the probable explanation is that in sleep people who are bound up in time in the waking state are able to escape its tentacles and see ahead more clearly. This is particularly likely to happen with those who have taught about religion or meditate deeply.

One of my communicators, Douglas Bader, has explained that the immediate next dimension dovetails into ours. After all, you couldn't have gaps between dimensions. There is therefore a lot of communication between our plane and the next, either consciously or subconsciously.

There are times when even I dismiss a glimpse of the future as 'just a dream', and live to regret it. One night, for instance, I dreamt I was in the country with my children and we were all gazing at a beautiful lake. Suddenly, the beauty of the scene was disturbed for me by the realization that we would all be stranded there, unable to get home. When I woke, I hardly gave my dream a second thought. The next day my son offered to take myself, my daughter, and our dog for a trip to the country in his car. It was a fine summer's day and we drove out of London in high spirits before stopping for a picnic. Then Thomas drove us on to a famous beauty spot, the Silent Pool in Surrey. We parked the car and started to walk through the woodland to the Silent Pool. When we got there I recognized it as the lake of my dream. But we'd arrived safely by car, now prosaically parked some distance away. It had got us there all right and was working perfectly; I felt a little uneasy but dismissed the feeling.

When we set off for home, the car started with no problems.

But we had gone only a few yards when it began to make alarming noises. My daughter, who is a trained car mechanic, said it sounded serious and advised Thomas to pull off the road as she thought it sounded as though the manifold had gone. Thomas pulled into a layby and Georgina leapt out of the car and went round to peer under the bonnet. She announced it *was* the manifold that was causing the trouble but that she could fix it if Thomas had some tools in the car. He didn't, so we had to walk down the road to find a telephone to ring the AA and ask them to come and rescue us. Thomas suggested that we needn't all wait for the AA, so Georgina and I had a hunt around and found a bus route. We took the dog with us and caught a bus to the nearest railway station. Then we caught a train to London, and another train out to South London where I live. As for Thomas, eventually the AA arrived and towed his car into a garage in Guildford from where he made his own way home by train.

A leisurely trip out into the country on a sunny summer's day had turned into an exhausting trek for home! We weren't really stranded, of course, as we were able to get back, but you could say we were temporarily stuck and the car was definitely stranded. On the way home I more than once thought of my dream and wished I'd paid more attention to it.

But I still don't try to see into the future because if I saw something dreadful ahead I'd be living in awful apprehension until it happened, and if I saw something marvellous I'd probably be living only for the future, and I would miss so much by not paying sufficient attention to what is actually happening now. I believe you have to deal with things as they come along.

This is not just my way of thinking, but the way I have been taught to think by my communicators beyond. Liszt doesn't tell me how to live my life, yet he is there if I need him. He wouldn't dream of trying to direct my life. He knows that I will learn far more from experiencing things myself, including my mistakes, than from him pointing me in the right direction.

All the time we are moulding our own future: by what we say, write, do, and by our thoughts. Other people will influence our life unless we have achieved a supreme state of inner control and balance. There are very few people who are in total control like this, either in this world or in the next, but I am sure there are some very advanced souls like this who are helping the world with their thoughts and prayers.

I am trying to develop along these lines. I try to work in the present because I believe that what I'm doing now, what I'm thinking now, is affecting my future and that of other people around me. So I have to keep concentrating on this one point entirely, the point of now. From there will flow my future and that of others. I know I could possibly look into the future but I choose not to try.

Of course, looking into the future is a fascination with many people, and a lot of people make money out of fortune-telling. I am sure some fortune-tellers are talented people who are forced into this line of work to make a living, but I am also sure that others have no talents at all and are just taking a lot of people for a ride. They are kept in business by some people's obsession with the need to know. It's sad when people are so preoccupied with the future that they fail to learn from the present. An enquiring mind is an asset, but too much preoccupation with either the past or the future can be disorienting.

I used to go every Friday to a psychic centre in London. I attended it as a means of investigating into the whole psychic system, and the different ways of utilizing psychic abilities, and to find which of these I could use most proficiently. There were several mediums working in the building in Belgrave Square, and a reception office to allocate clients to us. We would go to our allotted rooms and wait to be consulted. We knew nothing about our clients; not even their names. Sometimes it is difficult to work under such conditions, but I found that very often spirits would turn up with messages for my clients, usually to offer comfort to the bereaved.

But a large percentage of these sitters obviously only wanted fortune-telling. People would ask whether their Aunt Mary was going to leave her money to them, where they should go for their holidays, whether their husbands or wives would leave them, and all sorts of ridiculous material things. They were treating me like an agony aunt and I feel mediumship isn't meant for that sort of counselling. To me, these gifts are sacred and I feel they should be dedicated to the service of God in the highest possible way, not be exploited for material gain or petty issues.

I had to tell my clients that I wasn't there to solve their problems or tell them which path in life to take, merely to provide a line between bereaved people and the ones who had gone. In my opinion, their needs would often have been met by a sympathetic priest or family doctor. It was really a great shame for them that the only person they could turn to was a stranger in a psychic centre. I believe that church-based counselling, if it were more widely available, could perform a very valuable function for these people.

It was just too risky for me to answer questions as to whether Aunt Mary was going to leave her money to a favourite nephew, for instance. Suppose I got the answer, 'Yes, she is going to leave you all her money, and it will be a considerable amount.' To take the worst possible consequence, the man might have been sufficiently avaricious and unscrupulous to think: Well, I'll do away with Aunt Mary, then. Such fortune-telling might have opened up all sorts of dreadful possibilities.

Sometimes people would come in and ask me if they would win the pools that week, or even what they should put down as the score draws. I found it all rather degrading, and didn't do it for very long before I resigned. I was only doing it as an investigation, but I quickly became disillusioned! I should stress that I don't think it is wrong to do the pools, and have even had a little bit of luck in that direction myself. After my husband died, when money for myself and my children was in short supply, I worked as a school dinner lady. During the school holidays, we were paid a retainer but it wasn't really enough to live on. Liszt knew I was worried and suggested I try the football pools. He certainly didn't assist me with the form-filling, but I sent off my coupon and duly received through the post a dividend of £10 – not an enormous amount, but enough to see me through the Easter holidays.

Then, as Christmas drew nearer, I was again worried about money for Christmas food and presents for the children. Liszt suggested, with a twinkle in his eye, that I might try the football pools again. I took his advice and this time the dividend was £51. It was, for me, a very big miracle – particularly as I do not make a practice of filling in football coupons. Perhaps Liszt himself did not know that I would win, but simply had a hunch that I might.

People have often asked me if I can foretell gambling wins, and the answer is no. In the normal way, the spirit world will have nothing to do with an assistance towards monetary gain. If they did, I might by now be a very rich woman indeed. But everything I have – my tiny flat in South London, furniture and a few possessions – I have worked for, and earned. I think it's a far better feeling to think, 'I worked for this, I deserve it,' rather than, 'What luck this just landed at my feet.'

Something Liszt once said has always stayed in my memory. When someone asked me to look into the future for them because they wondered what course of action to take, Liszt said somewhat ruefully, 'The spirit world should not be treated like an advice bureau, nor should it be used to sort out people's emotional tangles. The right function of the spirit world is to uplift people's consciousness, to help them to turn towards the light.'

POEMS

By now you will have gathered that I don't receive communications only from the classical composers. I have been in touch with pop stars, politicians, philosophers and public figures of all kinds. I have also received a fairly substantial body of work from some very well-known poets, including Emily Brontë, Elizabeth Barrett Browning, Rupert Brooke, William Blake, Samuel Taylor Coleridge, John Keats, Edward Lear, Percy Bysshe Shelley and William Wordsworth. My latest, very welcome, poetic visitor is Sir John Betjeman.

A spirit with whom I seem to enjoy a special rapport is that of William Wordsworth. I believe we share a very similar outlook, arising from our deep underlying religious faith, and I have always seen his later poetry at least as reflecting these Christian hopes and beliefs.

Strangely, for an inhabitant of the next world, Wordsworth's appearance is rather older than that of many spirits. He has the light grey hair and a slightly lined face of a hale and hearty man in his early fifties or so. Most of the spirit visitors appear to be in their twenties or thirties, so obviously Wordsworth is an exception in that respect.

He has a very proper, rather drilled and schoolmasterly way of speaking, and will always greet me punctiliously and politely.

He told me that though he wrote so much in this life, his work was not achieved in the spontaneous manner of so many of his fellow poets. He carefully selected each word before committing it to paper. He was always conscious of striving after the perfect form as well as the *mot juste*, and the precision of his written work closely echoes the exactness of his speech.

I remember John Keats as a rather different, very intense sort of character. I haven't seen him for a while now but I can remember the sensation of brooding which seemed to emanate from him. This wasn't a malign or frightening force at all, but he told me that even in the next life, as so often in this, he has a tendency to look back instead of enjoying the present. He realizes that this was one of his greatest failings in life, but he wasn't always able to help himself, blessed though he was with some devoted friends. Often he was in the grip of ferocious depressions, or 'dark moods', which probably resulted at least in part from his weakened physical state.

In appearance he is small and slight, and appeared to me to be very slightly hunchbacked, or at least very high-shouldered. He had a swarthy, olive-toned complexion and looked to me to be in his late thirties – a little surprisingly, considering that he left this life aged 26. Obviously, like Wordsworth's, his soul is a quite mature one. He didn't have a handsome face; it was the sort you could pass by in a crowd and not think twice about, but alone in a room with him I did feel a force and intensity to his character which was very arresting.

Of the female poets, I like Emily Brontë very much, and have seen her recently. She has a delightfully mercurial personality and talking to her is easy and fun. She much resembles the famous portrait of her together with her two sisters, although I have never met either of them. She says that the whole family is now reunited in spirit, and their lifetime differences ironed out. Apparently, in this life, she always felt the odd one out of the sisters. I suppose with three people one is always destined to feel this way, but Emily tells me that she was undoubtedly her father's favourite and sometimes that led to difficulties with her sisters in this life.

Elizabeth Barrett Browning is another delightful occasional visitor. The popular image of her as the beautiful but suppressed invalid is not far from the truth, I suppose, but it doesn't do much justice to the strength of her personality. She is certainly very lovely, with a fair-skinned oval face, long curling eyelashes and dark ringlets. She has a willowy figure and her deportment is very graceful.

Although in this life she was cowed and kept down by her father, she did in fact inherit a measure of his iron will. She needed to, in order to survive. I also sense very developed powers of concentration within her; presumably she needed these in order to work where and when she could in that repressive household. Still, it's odd to hear from the lips of that graceful beautiful woman a note of unmistakable command in the voice which is probably a quite unconscious echo of her father's authoritative tones.

I'm very fond indeed of the spirit of John Betjeman from whom an irresistible aura of *bonhomie* and good-heartedness emanates. Of his work, he once said to me, 'You know, I wrote some of my poetry in quite a slapdash fashion, and I didn't bother to change it!' But, slapdash or not, it has a highly enjoyable feeling to it which I believe stemmed from the poet's own great curiosity and enjoyment of daily life. He was constantly watching and observing in this life, so interested in even the most commonplace of things and people that seemed to speak volumes to him. He tells me he had a great feeling that the so-called 'common man' wasn't really everyday and ordinary at all, but that each and every person he met was a minor miracle in their own right.

When writing, he often wished there were more words to play around with. He often had to splash out into some quite ludicrous terms in order to convey his precise meaning. He knows some people laughed at his poetry but thinks: Better to have been laughed at than not to have been read at all. He tells me that he loved reading in this life, a wide and catholic range of authors, sometimes having as many as 16 books on the go at one time. I didn't believe this at first, but on closer acquaintance with his enthusiasm and vivacity, I'd say it was quite possible.

Some poets are more frequent visitors than others, but I have certainly not received the quantity of work from the poet visitors that I have from the composers. I believe that the poets learned there was a link through me to this world and that they therefore arranged for a few representative samples of their work to reach me.

I very much enjoyed taking down these poems and hope that there are few, if any, errors in transmission. I am not naming the poets responsible for each poem for several reasons. First, because the poets' main concern in sending me new works was not to reinforce their earthly reputations but to present our world with new poems for our entertainment and enjoyment. They hope in this way to stimulate and provoke an appreciation of poetry which they have been sad to see slipping away during the past few decades.

Another reason why I have not identified the poet's work in each case is because I know that if I do I may be besieged by a fresh army of experts, literary this time instead of musical, who will insist on examining each work as evidence for or against my claim to be in communication with the poets, and who will demand more and more evidence to fuel the controversy. I have been through the same tedious process of trying to satisfy public and expert opinion with endless details of proof in the case of the composers, and I do feel once is enough.

I believe that anyone with an interest in poetry could happily spend a few hours or so studying the poems and trying to work out which poet was responsible for which. Appendix 3 contains 24 poems by the ten poets named in the first paragraph of this chapter, so obviously some poets are represented more than once. Why not read them through and try to fit the poets to the poems? Even if you don't succeed, I'd like to think you will still enjoy the poetry for its own sake.

Incidentally, the lovely sonnet 'Hope' was set to music in the after-life for Kathleen Ferrier, the great contralto, to perform there. The poet was not a close contemporary of hers, though. Now, no more clues.

PAINTINGS

Many years ago I had a friend, living nearby, who was rather lonely and shy. She wanted to go to an evening class and asked me if I would go with her. I agreed, but was a bit taken aback when she said she had enrolled us in an art class. I had never been any good at art, and in fact had been thrown out of that class at grammar school for 'inconsistent work'. But I didn't want to let my friend down so we went along.

Most of the people there were absolute beginners, many of them retired, so I didn't feel uncomfortable at my own intrinsic lack of ability. We started off by drawing in pencil, and I was pretty average. Well, to be truthful, somewhat below average. Then we moved on to drawing with charcoal. Using charcoal, I felt a lot easier and I enjoyed myself more than I had in previous weeks. I was aware that I was receiving some kind of inspiration from the other side, but I thought it was friendly spirits trying to put me at ease. They knew I hadn't really wanted to be there in the first place, and every week I got nervous about not being very good at the work.

I was having a lovely time working on my large charcoal drawing while the art teacher wandered around the room, looking at our efforts and trying to give us help. When she got to my drawing-board, she just stared in amazement with her mouth open. Eventually, she said, 'That's Samuel Palmer.' I asked who he was, and she told me he was a famous painter with a distinctive style. I had never heard of him, and I wasn't consciously aware of him communicating through me when I was doing the charcoal drawing. But my efforts that week were leagues ahead of what I had previously produced, and the teacher was happy enough, even though my work wasn't 'all my own'! She thought her teaching talents had enabled me to improve in just a few weeks of evening classes!

It took me back to my years at school when sometimes I was praised for my excellent drawing, but at others just couldn't produce the same level of work. Obviously, at times I was being helped; at others I wasn't. But my teacher called me to the front of the class, pronounced me inconsistent and lazy, and forbade me to attend any more classes. Fortunately for me, my evening-class teacher didn't take the same high moral tone on the weeks when inspiration was lacking on my part.

Samuel Palmer inspired me for quite a few works, before I actually saw him. I think he wanted the authenticity of his work to be confirmed to me by a third party before he communicated directly. I found him a pleasant enough, Victorian-looking gentleman but I would guess he had quite a temperamental side to him in this life.

Apart from Samuel Palmer's communications, I also received inspiration from Turner – usually in watercolour – some wonderfully authentic Blake drawings, and many other oddments from a host of different artists. The marvellous thing about this period was that I couldn't identify for myself which artist was communicating through me. I would just carry on with the drawing or painting, and it wouldn't be until the art teacher or someone else said, 'Oh, that's Van Gogh!' that I would know who was guiding me.

I found Vincent Van Gogh surprisingly easy and affable to talk to. In fact, he sat quite willingly for me to attempt a portrait of him: blue eyes, red hair and *both* ears. My impression was that in this life he was a very tense, taut sort of character. Inspiration came in great waves, when he would be working feverishly against the clock as at other times he just couldn't produce the same work, which led to bouts of intense depression.

One of the most interesting artist visitors was a striking figure indeed. He seemed to be quite old for a spirit, looking to be in his sixties or so, with fine ascetic features, exquisite hands and deep-set dark eyes. He was dressed in a full-length sleeveless over-mantle and wide-sleeved robe, and wore miraculously shiny, pointed-toe shoes which didn't seem to be of leather. There were expensive-looking rings on his fingers, and the whole impression his appearance gave was of wealth and discernment. When I asked his name, he just said 'Lorenzo', from which I gathered he was Italian, but not much else. Through me, he painted some exquisite circular miniatures of tiny flowers. Every time I saw him I tried to extract a bit more information from him. Eventually, he told me his surname was di Credi, his date of birth 1456, and the year he passed over, 1537.

I asked a friend of mine, Mrs Elizabeth Parrott, who is a professional artist, if she could find out anything about him. She delved through her books but whenever I saw her she still hadn't been able to trace anything about my friend Lorenzo. She was just about to give up the search when she found a tiny entry connected with the Florentine court of the time. It just said Lorenzo di Credi, artist, and gave the dates he had given me. I was delighted, most of all because he was so obscure. It proved that I wasn't just trying to latch on to the famous artists!

My artist's period didn't last very long. Unfortunately, I had to drop painting and drawing because, with music, healing, and the many other things I have to do in my life, I just don't have the time. My friend died and I didn't see any point in carrying on the Art classes without her. I did start to paint at home but I have a very small flat and it just wasn't practical to leave all my artist's paraphernalia lying about. And I had absolutely nowhere to keep the finished paintings, so I gave most of my pictures away: the Palmers, the Turners, the Van Goghs. But I kept one. Over the rocking chair in my flat, I have hung a 'Van Gogh'. Well, actually, it is signed 'Rosemary Brown', but I know for certain it was inspired by Van Gogh.

GHOSTS, GUIDES, AND OTHER VISITORS

If Liszt or one of my other communicators appears to me, I see a spirit. A lot of people are under the mistaken impression that I see ghosts, but I see spirits – the difference being that to me a 'ghost' implies a duplicated image, whereas a 'spirit' means a soul living in spirit.

But what about all those stories of ghostly hauntings which repeat themselves over and over again? There are theatres which are supposed to have resident ghosts, country inns with extraterrestrial guests, and battle sites where spectral fighting rages. People go to great lengths, camping out all night sometimes in cold places, trying to catch glimpses of these phenomena. What exactly are they seeing?

In a few cases, a spirit may frequent a place where it has been very happy or very sad, or the victim of some terrible tragedy. But there seems no doubt that many so-called hauntings are only echoes from the past. Violent or tragic events become indelibly imprinted on their surroundings, creating the right atmosphere for a ghostly haunting. These apparitions and ghostly noises are merely kinds of projected images and recorded soundwaves which continue to echo through time.

The science of psychometry shows that material objects can carry with them a history of their past. I, for instance, can handle an object and immediately receive impressions of what it was used for, even by whom. If small material objects can contain their own history it would follow that buildings, or even urban areas or country sites, can do the same. No wonder, then, that in certain places there is a definite sensation of the continuing presence, but it is not a spirit presence in the true sense of the word. Nowadays, we are all familiar with television programmes. These may be repeats or have been pre-recorded, though when we watch them they might seem to be live broadcasts. Hauntings which are merely displaying previous happenings are rather similar to those TV repeats; they relate old histories, old emotions, old events.

It is interesting to consider how we can tell the difference between these echoes from the past and manifestations which are actually taking place here and now. One good test to find out whether a spirit is actually present, as opposed to its echo or shadow, is to see whether it can react to the present; for instance, whether it is aware of its surroundings, aware of being observed, or, more conclusively, whether the spirit can actually converse with us. Instead of being static images, or images moving in a pre-determined fashion, real spirits are living, animated souls, capable of movement and speech. Liszt has responded when I have tried to draw him by sitting in a chair in my lounge and striking up a pose which he thought presented his best profile!

It may not always be easy to distinguish a living spirit from a ghostly echo, as occasionally a spirit may be out of touch with our present time and unable to react to us. Liszt once said to me, 'There are spirits who are living souls, and there are shadows of ghosts.' It's like saying there are people on earth, and there are their shadows thrown from them by sunlight. The difference is that a person's shadow on earth flows from him, whereas ghost-shadows hover in the atmosphere unattached to any living spirit-soul.

The universe is full of echoes. Everything that ever took place is recorded somewhere, somehow. These are sometimes known as the Akashic Records, and can occasionally be read or referred to by developed mediums or mystics, not in any material sense, but by a sort of mental 'plugging in' to a vast store of knowledge which could be likened to a huge computer bank in which the memory of everything that has ever happened is preserved.

When theosophists and others talk about the Astral Plane – which is commonly believed to be the next plane of existence –

as being a plane of illusion, they are probably basing their ideas on these psychic echoes, shadows and lingering after-images of the past. Some theosophists refer to 'empty astral shells' and draw the false conclusion that everything on the astral plane is unreal. I used to be a theosophist myself but found that sometimes their seeking after universal truth led them to draw over-simplistic conclusions – and sometimes to draw over-complicated ones!

On this subject, I found that Einstein wanted to communicate at some length. He revealed that

> All levels of existence have the essence of reality within them, otherwise they could not exist at all. There is an ultimate or fundamental level of reality which is behind all manifestations of energy, of life. This ultimate reality percolates through all levels, and without it everything would disintegrate. It is the binding force, the force which links all things. It is in all things, yet it is independent of all things. If all visible manifestations of it disappeared, it would still exist and could inaugurate a new series of manifestations.
>
> In other words, there are many areas of comparative reality; there are areas of comparative time and space. Most people can only deal with one level of reality at any given time, so all other levels remain closed to them. This often leads people to assume that any area other than the one they can perceive does not exist. This is a very limited conception which in the past has been widely adopted in scientific circles.

I have had contact with Einstein from time to time over the past few years. I think this isn't because he wants to contact me personally but because he would like to pass on some of his new thoughts to our world. There are many things, he says, that he would like to express in simple terms so that more people could understand them. But he admits that it is difficult to express some things in simple terms since by their very nature they are abstruse. The infinite, for instance, he says can be compared to a circle; it has no beginning and no end, yet it is not limited like a circle in circumference. It is an infinite circle. A notion, he says, which it is very difficult for the finite brain to envisage.

But to get back to our ghostly echoes. The expression 'astral shells' gives quite an apt description of the uninhabited spectral forms which linger on in some places. To see some of these astral shells is rather like reading a page in a history book. It gives you information about the past, not about the present. Like a video recording it gives you a re-run of a former event. Time moves on but the past remains suspended in a mysterious manner. One spirit bard put it like this:

> Images etched on the fabric of time dismay the
>   mortal eye with their appearances;
> The fearful shouts and cries of slaughtered souls
>   hang in the air like vapours undispersed.
> Terrors of the past resound where they first
>   engendered.
> Deeds and misdeeds alike bear endless witness to
>   themselves.

The bard shall remain nameless lest I stir up a whole lot of controversy about his identity, but he mischievously insisted I refer to him thus: 'Call me Will, if you will, but if I be not Will, what will you call me?'

Many people ask me about the spirit guides who either speak through mediums when they are entranced, or give 'inspired' addresses through them. I have found these guides a very mixed bunch. Occasionally I have come across one who is full of wisdom and understanding, and I have heard some 'inspired' addresses which have been genuinely inspired and inspiring. But I have also come across a number of guides who I suspect are no more than secondary personalities of the medium in question.

I have come into contact, both directly and indirectly, with so-called guides who have been downright ignorant and completely lacking in any compassion. I have witnessed the outpourings of guides who are more like overweening egotists than anything else, and who take it upon themselves to deliver unkind and unhelpful tirades, and totally unjustified censure. I have to stress that some mediums have good guides, guides they have learned to trust and who help their work enormously.

After a number of disillusioning experiences I have become very wary of guides in general and trust only the spirits in the beyond who have proved themselves to me to be reliable and of good intention. In some ways I suppose Liszt has acted as a guide, in the way that a best friend would advise and help you, always there but not overpowering you. But I would not claim him as my guide. If I need guidance, I always look to God.

There are many apparently strange phenomena in our world: blunt razor blades left overnight inside a cardboard model of a pyramid are found to be sharp again by morning; a Leningrad housewife can make a compass revolve by looking at it; Yuri Geller can bend forks by staring at them; another Russian housewife can separate the white of a broken egg from the yolk by staring at it, and a lady from a village in the Urals can read with her elbow! How much more is there for us to learn of and marvel at? It is no use turning our backs on these matters and saying we don't want to know. Someone, some time, is going to investigate them, and we had better be prepared for startling news about the latent powers of our own beings and the untapped range of energy waves.

These phenomena are fascinating, and they cannot always be explained. I have grown accustomed, throughout my life, to things happening that might seem strange to other people. They are little events which other people might these days refer to as 'things that go bump in the night'!

Apart from the clairvoyance, clairaudience, and other aspects of what is known as mental mediumship, there have been occasional manifestations of a more physical nature. Perhaps it is a pity that such manifestations are not more common so that a greater number of people could experience psychic activities at first hand. On the other hand, such experiences might prove spine-chilling to the uninitiated!

Occasionally, I have witnessed myself the movements of earthly objects or heard with my own ears sounds that were clearly not accountable to 'natural causes'. One of these manifestations took place when I was in my teens and was having a discussion with a school friend about religion. This friend of mine had been brought up in a Roman Catholic convent, a place where the fear of God and the devil and hellfire had been driven deep into the poor girl's mind. She was a nervous wreck because she was only too aware – as any honest person is – of her own shortcomings. She lived in constant dread of the hellfire she was convinced must await her after death.

I tried to give her some peace of mind, and to mitigate some of the harm done to her by the teaching to which she had been subjected. She asked me whether I believed in another life, and I replied that I not only believed but was sure of it because I had seen my own brother and conversed with him after his death. I told her that he had assured me, since his passing, that God is a being of infinite love, and not the vengeful punishing deity misrepresented to her.

My friend sat beside me on the settee in front of the hearth. She stared into the flames and said how awful it was to think that one day she would be cast into flames of everlasting fire. 'Nonsense!' I cried. 'You must put that idea right out of your mind. It is not true. God would not do a thing like that; if He did, He would not be a God of love, mercy and compassion. God loves you. He loves us all, although we are not perfect.' 'Oh! I wish I could believe that God loves me,' my friend cried, wringing her hands in desperation. 'I wish your brother could give me some sign to show me that I won't go to Hell when I die.'

I was appalled to see such damage done to a young, sensitive mind. It seemed that my friend would go through life tormented by fear. Silently, I prayed for her to be helped, and for her to understand the great depth of God's tender, all-enfolding love. Suddenly, we were both startled by a loud tapping sound coming from the mantelpiece. We looked up and watched spellbound as a large, weighty vase, which stood in the centre, moved backwards and forwards, striking the mirror behind it. It struck the mirror three times altogether, then returned to its central position and was still.

For a moment, my friend and I were silent, speechless at this strange happening. Then she suddenly burst out, 'It was a sign!

It was the sign I had prayed for, the sign of the Holy Trinity. Don't you see, the vase struck three times, the number of the Trinity. I was praying to God the Father, God the Son, and God the Holy Ghost for help, and that was the answer to my prayer.' She fell on her knees, weeping quietly, and stammering, 'God be praised. He heard me . . . He answered me.'

Was it my brother in spirit, knocking the vase against the mirror? Was he aware of her distress, of her dire need for reassurance, and had he caused the manifestation to give her comfort? Or was it a divine intervention in response to her desperate prayers? Whatever or whoever produced the phenomenon, it was certainly miraculous in the effect it had on my friend. From being a trembling, fearful person, she changed into a radiantly self-confident young woman, assured of God's loving care for her.

I wonder sometimes where she is now. If she ever reads this, I would like to tell her that I have that vase to this day, and whenever I look at it, I am reminded of the 'sign from Heaven' which freed her from her burden of fear. Her name was Mary McGowan, and she lived in Streatham and went to my school. I expect she married young – she was a pretty girl, and I hope she has had a happy life.

I must say that vase has never behaved like that since! But we possessed one object which often behaved in a strange manner. This was the old reconditioned piano that I managed to acquire several years after the war. It began to do its tricks in my mother's time. She and I would be sitting quietly, sipping our afternoon tea in broad daylight, talking of little everyday matters, when the piano would suddenly decide to play!

The lid over the keyboard was often left open, as my mother had a theory that it was better for the piano, keeping it 'aired' in some way. We would sit and watch the notes of the keyboard going up and down as if being pressed by unseen fingers. Liszt told me in later years that he was responsible, since he was trying to attract my attention.

Some years after my mother had passed away, my daughter was unable to sleep one night. She told me the next morning that she decided to get up and make herself some tea. Her brother and I were fast asleep in our respective bedrooms. She brewed some tea and sat drinking it in the kitchen at the back of the house, with our dog and cat beside her, when she heard several chords being played quite loudly on the piano which was in a room towards the front of the house. Thinking I had come down from my bedroom and begun to play, she went to the room to ask me if I would like a cup of tea – and the room was empty!

She found I was still asleep in bed, two flights of stairs above, in the front part of the house. We reasoned it out that had a mouse been responsible, it might have possibly made some slight sound, although I doubt whether the weight of a mouse could produce so much as one *pianissimo* note! But a mouse certainly could not play chords loudly. We presumed that Liszt was the performer.

This story had a remarkable sequel. When I moved out of the large old house which was the family heritage, I had to go into a very much smaller residence. By this time, a kind and generous benefactor had presented me with a small upright piano, and there was scarcely room for one piano, let alone two in my new home. I was obliged to dispose of the old piano, and it became the property of a friend of mine with a spacious house three storeys high.

The piano had been installed in her house for about six months when it gave cause for alarm. My friend had a lodger in her house, a young man who is a Roman Catholic, and he was the witness in this case to the activity of the 'haunted piano'. One night, when he was unable to sleep, he heard a chord, not just a single note, played clearly and distinctly on the piano though everyone else in the house was in bed asleep. He said he was so scared that he almost rushed out of the house.

My friend related the incident to me a few days later when we met, and said they had teased the lodger by saying he must have had too much spirit of the alcoholic type. He denied flatly that he had had anything to drink, and said he knew he had not imagined it because he is not given to flights of imagination. He did not know at the time, neither did my friend, that the piano had acquired the habit of playing itself – or of being played by ghostly fingers. I had made no mention of the phenomenon when the piano changed hands as I was under the impression that the ghostly playing only took place in my old home. I did not expect the ghostly pianist to be transferred with the pianoforte.

My mother and I often witnessed an unusual phenomenon in our old house at Balham. On the landing, there was a row of about half a dozen hooks on which we used to hang our coats. We would loop our coats neatly over the hooks – but when next we went to fetch our coats, we would find the loops wound over and over so tightly that we had a job to get the coats off. This happened repeatedly, and my mother took it as a joke on the part of some spirit. In fact, I later learned from her that she'd had a younger brother who died as a small child. Perhaps it was his childish spirit's idea of a game. We even tried to wind our coats on to the hooks in the same way, but found it completely impossible. There was obviously no means by which human agency could get those loops twisted into so many tightlywound coils.

This particular phenomenon was all the more fascinating because it used to follow us wherever we went. We would find our coats with the loops twisted into umpteen coils in the houses of other people whom we visited, much to the mystification of our hosts or hostesses. Once, after my father had passed away, my mother and I took a week's holiday at Christchurch, where we stayed in a small guest-house. We hung our coats on hooks on the back of our door. Sure enough, the same thing happened there, and my mother said, 'The fairies have come with us.' Since she has passed away, this phenomenon has ceased, so it must have been linked with her.

FAIRIES AND ANGELS

When you were a child, you believed in fairies at the bottom of the garden, didn't you? What made you stop believing in them? Somewhere along the line you must have been conditioned into thinking that it was a childish notion and it was much more grown-up to boast you didn't believe in them any more. Now I'm quite grown-up, yet I still believe in them. I know there are fairies at the bottom of the garden because I have seen them.

There are so many stories about fairies, pixies, elves, call them what you will, you wonder how they began. Don't you think that some time ago there must have been some grounds for believing in the existence of such creatures? Nursery rhymes and children's books are scattered with them, pantomimes have their fair share, and ballets are often filled with the traditional good fairies and bad fairies, water sprites and other ethereal beings. Composers have even written music about them. Grieg, for instance, with his trolls in the 'Hall of the Mountain King', while Wagner simply revelled in supernatural creatures: giants, dwarfs, *Nibelungen*, and goodness knows what else.

We also meet with fairy beings in literature. Shakespeare immediately springs to mind, with the fairy folk in *A Midsummer Night's Dream*, and the spirit Ariel in *The Tempest*. And do you remember the mysterious story, 'Mary Rose', by J. M. Barrie, in which an enchanted island was peopled with fairies? There are numerous stories of banshees, gnomes, leprechauns, sprites, naiads, nymphs, dryads and sylphs. They turn up everywhere, in every country. There are the kelpies in Scotland; the Little People in Ireland; peris in Persia and the Lorelei in Germany.

In the Hindu religion there is a belief that every mountain, tree and so on has its own supernatural spirit. Those of us who are old enough can remember how gremlins were blamed for aircraft troubles during the Second World War. There also were many yarns about the sirens which lured sailors to their deaths. But on the other hand, there is the world-famous fairy godmother who comes to put everything right. Is it just that we delight in inventing such creatures, or is there some truth in the stories? So widespread and persistent are the legends that one really might begin to think there's no smoke without fire.

Psychologists would probably say that we are creating these various kinds of supernatural being as a projection of our own many-sided natures. One thing is certain: literature, music and art would all be the poorer without them. And what if, far from a creation of our subconscious, they were in fact the product of a race memory, the remnants of a time when man and the spirits of nature were forced to be much closer and more inter-dependent?

I have more than a suspicion that there are some kinds of elemental being, usually living close to nature. And I am not the only person by a long shot who thinks I've seen some of them. Of course, people think you are crazy if you admit it. But let me tell you this little anecdote which made our family think twice before dismissing such creatures as figments of our imagination.

As a small child, one of my brothers often talked of a little green man who used to come and sit at the foot of his bed. My mother, and the rest of the family, including me, just dismissed it as a childish fantasy. But one winter's day, when we were all sitting round the fire, I was startled to see a gnome-like creature who was obviously sharing the warmth.

He was dressed entirely in green, with a green hat on his head, and I have to admit he looked very much like the ornamental gnomes you sometimes see in suburban gardens. I was so astonished that I blurted out, 'I can see a gnome.' I described the little man and my brother said it sounded just like the little green man he used to see. Parapsychologists might explain the whole thing as a mind picture which I had picked up from my brother. But, wait, there is more.

After my brother married, he moved to a new house in Surrey. His wife did not believe in spirits or 'any of that sort of rubbish'. However, she was in for a shock. One day, soon after my brother had left the house for work, his wife went into their bedroom to make the bed. She opened the door and saw, sitting on the radiator just inside the room, a little green man. The same little green man from our childhood. Evidently he was a great one for warmth! My sister-in-law was scared stiff and, though the little green man grinned at her, she ran to the telephone and called my brother at work to say: 'You must come home, straight away.' She described the little green man to my brother, who said, 'Oh, it's only him. He won't harm you.'

It took my sister-in-law quite a while to come to terms with what she had actually seen, but of course it did open her mind to thinking that maybe there was something in 'that sort of rubbish' after all. What struck us as rather strange about the incident was that the little man had decided to move with my brother to his new home. It was as if there was some kind of bond between him and my brother. Or perhaps he liked my brother's modern house much better than the old family home.

When I was a very small child, I remember staring at a large pink rose we had standing in a vase on the sideboard. We had no garden so flowers in the house were something of a rarity. I stood in front of it, just gazing at its loveliness. Suddenly I saw a beautiful fairy face in the centre of the rose, smiling gently out at me. I rushed out of the room to fetch my mother. 'Come quick, come quick,' I shouted, 'there's a fairy in the rose.' My mother followed me into the room, no doubt just to humour me, but, alas, when we got to the rose there was no longer any sign of the lovely smiling face. Did I see it, or was I seeing things? The sweet smile on the fairy face inside the flower has remained vivid in my memory until this day.

Another time I remember seeing a cloud of tiny multi-coloured fairies round a bunch of bluebells. They weren't all blue, as one might have expected, and were human in form though they had wings, two. They were tiny. And sometimes, when taking a stroll in the countryside, I have caught glimpses of other fairy creatures.

A few years ago, I met a musician in Edinburgh who seemed a very down-to-earth and serious-minded man. His name was Ogilvie Crombie and he used to give talks about the nature spirits he has seen. He spoke so sincerely and seriously that you felt that what he had to say just had to be true. He passed on a few years after we met but I always marvelled at the way he had the courage to speak out publicly about his experience.

From my own experience, which has been limited to sightings only with no spoken communication, I would say that such fairy creatures are a different line of evolution from that of the spirit world. They belong to a different order of things entirely – the so-called Devic System – and have strong lines with the natural world. Which is why, if you believe in fairies, you should join the fight to protect their natural countryside habitat. I believe that Wordsworth probably communed with these nature spirits, for the living power of Nature can be strongly felt in his work.

I have also seen angels, although it is not necessary always to see them to know that they are present. For instance, if I am healing or praying there may suddenly be a wonderful indescribable atmosphere of peace around me and I will know that an angel is present. Like the fairies, angels belong to a separate line of evolution; they have some points of similarity with the human race, but they are not part of it. The angelic system appears to be a hierarchical one, some angels possessing very much more power than others.

The healing angels, for instance, are enormous beings – they seem to me to be about 20 feet tall – and are obviously very powerful indeed. They are also very beautiful and appear to be swathed about with glorious soft pastel-coloured material. This isn't a dress or robe but is actually a part of their aura. They seem to have arms and wings which they will extend above the sufferer, but they do not always appear to have feet. Their faces are human in form but their expression of serenity has never been matched in my experience by any human being's. I can feel an air of great power and compassion emanating from them, but not emotion in the human sense.

There are higher angels still. On at least two occasions I have been in the presence of the Archangel Michael, and the experiences were so vivid and intense that they will remain with me always. I didn't *see* him in the sense I did the healing angels, but I could recognize his distinct and individual presence around me and the almost unbearable joy it evoked in me was like nothing I had felt before. In his presence, you feel very close to God.

I have also seen the Angel Gabriel, and on this occasion my husband Charles, who was then alive, shared the experience. We had not been married long and were quietly at home together one evening when I became aware of an angel standing in the corner of the room. I did not wish to alarm Charles but, to my astonishment, after Gabriel had introduced himself, Charles volunteered that, though I might think him quite mad, he believed he could see the Angel Gabriel. I reassured him that I could see the angel, too, and Gabriel's purpose in coming soon became clear.

He is the angel most associated with birth and death – that is, with transitions. I have often seen him beside the bed of the dying, and sometimes in the company of a mother-to-be. In this case, although we had not realized it yet ourselves, *I* was the mother-to-be. Some months later, I gave birth to a little girl.

Another close relative of mine had direct experience of an angel. An uncle, Leigh Vincent Scott Sugg, was present at the Battle of Mons in the First World War. Though cruelly wounded there – he suffered from an open wound in his abdomen for the rest of his life – he survived to tell the tale of the 'Angel of Mons', whom more than one soldier saw during the thick of the fighting. My uncle was a man without a shred of psychic ability and never again saw anything at all out of the ordinary terrestrial run of things, but he was quite convinced that he had seen the angel that day.

The iconography of angels in art is often rather formal and stiff-looking. In reality, they have a radiance and an inner beauty which I suppose are impossible for an earthly artist to capture.

A memorable experience of a holy presence came to me during a visit to Buckfast Abbey. The Abbey was full of sightseers and tourists. The friend with whom I was on holiday and I went into the east wing which contains a beautiful stained-glass window of Christ. We both sat still for a few moments of quiet thought and prayer. What happened next was one of the most overwhelmingly sacred experiences of my life. The chapel was quite full of people, yet in the midst of all that activity there was a stillness, a concentration of holiness and supreme love surrounding me. I find it impossible to describe my feelings properly in words.

I was deeply enfolded in intense love and compassionate acceptance. I felt I was in the presence of God Himself. That complete immersion in peace, love and joy was so vivid that the memory has never left me. It was one of those rare moments in life when we are lifted above the mundane into a place of consciousness that most of us do not even know exists. I could never doubt God's existence after that, and I know the experience has changed me.

Of course, I realize that to talk about the presence of angels and fairies is more or less asking for people to write me off as a crank. But I've stuck my neck out before, so here I go again. A few weeks ago I was lunching with a friend who has two young children, and her little boy lost his first tooth while I was there. He was full of how he was going to put it under his pillow that night, and wondered whether the tooth fairy would bring him 5p, 10p or maybe even run to 50p? His sister, who at eight is much older and wiser, of course, promptly informed him that there was no such thing as the tooth fairy so he might not get anything at all! As you can imagine, he was crestfallen. His mother said to him, 'You'll get something,' at which her daughter said: 'Yes, *you'll* put it under his pillow.' 'Will you, Mum?' asked her son. 'Is it you or is there a fairy?'

Poor Mum was struggling, so I stepped in and said, 'There *are* such things as fairies. I've seen them.' Both of the children turned and looked at me as if I were quite mad but I persisted, 'I've seen them lots of times,' and started to tell them about the fairy in the rose and the fairies dancing around the bluebells. Both children, including the doubting daughter, were enthralled. 'Tell us more,' they demanded when I had finished. Then they scooted down to the bottom of their garden to look for fairies.

I don't suppose they will ever see any, but I hope they never stop looking.

REINCARNATION

The subject of reincarnation fascinates many people and causes all sorts of controversy. I know people who would be horrified at the thought of having to return to this world again; on the other hand, there are those who would relish it.

One man said to me, 'How marvellous it would be to have another slice of life.' You can take it that he was having a good slice this time around, and wanted a second helping! But you can understand why people who have had immense suffering in their lives would prefer oblivion to further existence.

If reincarnation is the norm, as so many Far Eastern religions insist, it makes you wonder whether we have any say in the matter. Having worked in the civil service for many years, I can't help but get a certain mental picture of some sort of enormous bureaucratic celestial organization set up to deal with each case. I can visualize each person's papers being passed from desk to desk for assessment and ending up in the chief controller's in-tray awaiting a decision. Are the papers in order? One hopes so, lest a bureaucratic error sends someone packing back to earth when he or she should have been excused further duty!

It would be more likely that the whole process would take place automatically through simple cause and effect. It is that word 'simple' that is the key word. Cause and effect, as Einstein once said to me, are not always simple matters. There is rarely *one* cause and *one* effect. He said that causes tend to react on themselves and even cancel each other out. You can't really generalize, he added, because each situation of cause and effect contains variable factors: therefore the outcome cannot be predetermined. What Einstein says complicates the whole reincarnation issue. And it's complicated enough, whichever way you look at it!

If we have no choice about reincarnation, where does free will come into it all? That might not worry some Far Eastern people, who are often fatalistic in their outlook, but if there is an element of volition, what about the Christian element of free will? Is it that we volunteer to return to this world, with all its evils and suffering? Perhaps we might if we could see some worthwhile ultimate benefit.

And what about those people who might choose not to come back, but are needed here? People who, by their nature, have shown themselves to be the sort to bring about a better world. Could there really be a weeding out, or a department that sends back the good as well as the bad? Or is it, as the Eastern religions suggest, a question of sending back the unevolved to work their way, a level at a time, higher up the ladder towards the ultimate Nirvana?

The whole subject of reincarnation can be an immense distraction to us in our search for the ultimate good. It can so easily get us bogged down in the pursuit of personalities, or tempt the vain to seek self-aggrandisement in an alleged former incarnation as some illustrious personage. Liszt says that we, as individuals, are facets of our greater self. Each individual part exists in its own right, but forms part of a total self of which we are little aware; rather like each finger going together to make up a hand.

Reincarnation, Liszt tells me, is not a matter of one unit – that is, one individual – shuttling backwards and forwards between the spirit world and earth. But if you think of reincarnation as a group effort, as a team operating, he says that will give you a better idea of the process. He points out that if you consider the vast increase in the world's population, you can realize that it is statistically impossible that everyone on earth is a reincarnated soul. In fact, he says, it is misleading to speak of reincarnation as a personalized process.

Religious devotees in the beyond have explained that we

travel towards whatever plane of existence we identify with. If we identify strongly with material things we bind ourselves to them. We are then caught in the material plane until we change. It is only when we identify with God that we set foot on the pathway to freedom: freedom from self and its endless demands and desires. It is only when we are prepared to lose our lesser self in that greater self that we gain our spiritual freedom – which would mean our freedom from reincarnation, if there is such a thing.

Reincarnation is such a complicated matter that I don't think we will solve it in this world. Even experiments in regression under hypnosis have not so far brought forward absolutely conclusive results – except, of course, to those who are already convinced of reincarnation. Much of what is said under hypnosis in these experiments may be subconscious fantasizing, or picking up ancestral memories, race memories, or other bits of psychic flotsam and jetsam. One strange feature of regression under hypnosis is that the subject may claim to have lived in a country where the language spoken was completely unknown to the hypnotized person. Yet the subject does not seem to be able to speak in that language, in spite of apparently being able to recall every detail of a previous life in a foreign country.

I heard about an experiment that some scientists were conducting to investigate the possibilities of regression. They regressed a woman way back to the twelfth century, if I remember rightly. They asked her, while she was still under hypnosis, to describe what she was doing. She said she was in a kitchen in Devonshire, peeling potatoes. But of course potatoes had not yet been introduced to England. Next she said she was making jam and stirring the sugar in, but sugar had not been brought to England at that time, either! Which all goes to show, I think, that not all that is said under hypnosis fits in with the historical facts.

If people believe in reincarnation at least they believe in life after death, which no doubt gives them hope for better things to come and also a belief in some kind of central purpose in life. It might also act as a deterrent against crime because a prospective criminal might fear the consequences in a future existence.

Anything that will encourage people to lead better lives can't be totally without value: as Bertrand Russell reminded me the other day, most people still need the promise of a carrot or the threat of a penalty – or both – to induce good behaviour. And as there is a noticeable lack of both carrots and penalties these days, perhaps the theory of reincarnation will act as a deterrent to criminals.

I don't think myself that delving into past incarnations – even if they do exist, which I doubt – is a good idea. If, for instance, you found you had committed some horrible crime in a past life, you might well be bowed down by a sense of guilt. Or if you found that you had been some great person in a previous existence, you might well begin to give yourself airs and graces. Either way, what would be achieved? You could not undo your previous misdeed nor could your past glory raise you to present eminence. And how could you ever be absolutely sure that you were previously the person that a medium or spirit alleged?

I have been told by various mediums that I was once an Egyptian princess; that I was one of the oracles at Delphi; that I was Jane Seymour, wife of Henry VIII; that I was George Sand; that I was a pupil of Liszt (which somewhat clashes with being George Sand); that I *was* Liszt; that I was Chopin – how clever of me to have been both Liszt and Chopin! I have also been told that I was a French aristocrat, a Royalist in Cromwell's time, that I was one of Robin Hood's men, and so on *ad infinitum*. It seems I've been Old Uncle Tom Cobley and all – or is it Uncle Tom Cobblers and all? It does show that you have to take this kind of pronouncement with a large pinch of salt. And it's left me with the feeling that it is best to get on with our present lives and not go mooning after the past.

I personally do not care who I was, if I *was* ever somebody else! All I care about is what I am trying to become now, and that is more than a full-time task.

HEALING

During the last few decades tremendous advances have been made in medicine and surgery. We are also learning about the power of mind over body, and the effects of suggestibility. Through all this new research, one fact emerges clearly.

We've all heard it said about a sick person: 'He was determined to get well,' or 'He lost the will to live.' Without perhaps realizing what they are saying, people are acknowledging that the mind does have power over the body; in fact, a healing power. But is it the mind alone? Can anyone use this power? Do we need outside help? I believe we do not yet know much about the great healing force which exists in the universe, a force which could be described as the fountainhead of life, or, in other words, God. I believe that this healing power is available to everyone. It comes from God, either through the work of spirit-healers or through the more orthodox channels of doctors and nurses.

Churches offer prayers for the sick, sometimes with significant results, so obviously they believe that God has a hand in our health. Sadly, little laying-on of hands – the treating of illness by a process during which a healer touches the sick person – is practised by churches now. I say 'sadly' because there is so much emphasis laid on healing in the New Testament, with instructions to go out and heal the sick and comfort the bereaved.

Some people appear to have an inborn gift of healing; perhaps we all have the potential to heal others. I am sure we all have many potential gifts of which we are quite unaware. But the sheer necessity of coping with everyday life, of earning a living and having to deal with mundane matters gives little time for most of us to think about these things, let alone investigate them. As a dedicated Christian, I believe in God's power to heal us when we respond to that power. I think I have had proof that God answers prayers, and heals.

I don't think I can remember when I first learned to do healing. My mother used to heal by prayer but she never did laying-on of hands. Every evening at the same time, nine o'clock, she used to go to her room and pray. Then she would say out loud, or repeat mentally to herself, the names of people she knew who were ill. This is directional healing, where you concentrate on a particular person and try to link them in with the universal power of healing. She had some remarkable results: people who had terminal diseases made a complete recovery and went on to live another quarter of a century or more. Apparently, my mother's gifts in this direction were discovered when, as the young daughter of the house, she visited the poorer families of the neighbourhood. It was noticed that anyone with whom Miss Beatrice sat made a good recovery, even from killer diseases like diphtheria. And my mother never once fell ill from her contact with the sick. So it was mainly through her that I became aware of healing. She used to say 'You can join your prayers to mine to give more power,' so I began to work with her doing just that.

I think it was probably through my children that I became aware of my power of laying on hands. Once, when my son was very small, he came running in from the kitchen, his mouth gushing with blood. Somehow he had managed to cut the roof of his mouth very badly. I made a pad to try to stem the bleeding, then sat him on my lap, as any mother would, and held him close, saying over and over again, 'Please, God, stop the bleeding. Please, God, make him better.'

We sat like that for a time, my son gradually becoming calmer while I prayed for God's help. An hour later I took Thomas to the doctor's surgery when it opened. The bleeding had stopped, but I thought the doctor had better have a look at the wound. Our doctor could not believe that the accident had just happened. He said that in his view the injury must have happened at least 24 hours earlier because the wound was already beginning to heal. We came home with my son well on the way to recovery, and I was convinced that God had answered my prayers.

Often, my daughter would hurt her knee or something, and come to me and say, 'Please, Mummy, make it better.' I would put my hand over a cut or graze and sometimes I couldn't believe my own eyes. A wound would instantly seem to heal. I also did a lot of healing for my husband. Once he had a purulent tumour on the side of his face, and couldn't shave because of it. The doctor said he would have to have an operation to get rid of it, but my husband didn't like the idea of that, even though he was in terrible pain. Our doctor said it would have to be done immediately, and arranged for an ambulance to come and pick him up and take him into hospital for the operation. The two ambulance men duly arrived and tried to persuade my husband to go with them, but he was adamant. He said only force would get him to go.

As he was over 6 feet tall he wasn't a force the ambulance men fancied reckoning with, so they eventually went without him. My husband was in despair. He was in pain, he knew he had to have something done about the growth, but he had just sent away the ambulance. He pleaded with me to try to do something for him, so I started the laying-on of hands. In a short time, the tumour began to diminish and heal up, and after a few weeks it went completely.

When our doctor examined my husband's face he was absolutely amazed. He said it was extraordinary the way that new skin was growing over the place where the growth had been. I can't explain this sort of thing myself. It never ceases to amaze me. I do believe that there is a sort of healing power everywhere in the atmosphere and that, if we are attuned to it, it can work through us, especially if we approach it with the right attitude and motives. I think most people could do this sort of healing if they dedicated themselves to it.

On another occasion, my daughter came running to me with a dreadful splinter in her finger. She was crying with pain, and I began asking Christ to come and heal my daughter. I believe

Christ is total love and compassion, and I have always believed He would want to heal people, especially children. I believed He would come. Not that I would necessarily see Him, but that He would reach out and heal my daughter. I prayed and He came. Before my very eyes the splinter lifted itself out of my daughter's finger, and soon she was laughing and playing happily again.

Obviously, as the years have gone by, more and more people have become aware of my healing powers, although it is not something that I advertise. If people ask me to give them healing, I always advise them to seek the normal, more conventional, means to treatment as well. But a great many of the people who want my help have already tried all the usual treatments without relief.

One single person cannot take on too many patients. Regretfully, I can only take on very few as there are so many other demands on my time. One of the people who has asked me for healing is the celebrated cellist, Julian Lloyd Webber. In fact, he wrote about this in his book *Travels with My Cello*. But it is God's power that gives healing. I am only used as a link to convey the healing.

When he was 25 years old, Julian feared he would never play again because of awful pain in his finger. He had consulted specialists who could find nothing wrong, and various treatments failed. In desperation he came to my home in South London, and I massaged his finger. Julian says 'A feeling of great heat began to grow inside, and since that remarkable evening the pain has never returned.' I was also asked to help Julian when he had a kidney stone that even the doctors of Westminster Hospital didn't seem able to treat. I placed my hand near his kidney and prayed. Julian reported in his book: 'Suddenly the pain grew even more intense. The stone was already moving. Two hours later it had passed.'

Another friend of mine had had a round, flat, hard lump on her neck since childhood, initially about the size of an old halfpenny. It was a sebaceous cyst which gradually became badly infected and inflamed until it was about the size of a tangerine. She was advised by her doctor to have the cyst removed without delay, but was reluctant to have an operation as she had two young children under five. The doctor gave her a course of penicillin. The cyst was no longer infected but had not reduced in size at all. Then it began to discharge again.

After a further two weeks there was no improvement. I offered to help, and after the first healing session the cyst was immediately reduced in size. Within ten days, after several more healing sessions, the swelling had gone down, leaving merely a small discoloration of the skin. Finally, and most remarkably of all, the cyst disappeared after my friend had had it for 25 years.

I have helped the same lady's husband with healing for various troubles. A few years ago he went to see an osteopath for a back problem. On this occasion, the treatment was completed with some rather aggressive neck manipulation and clearly something went wrong. Rather than a click on one side, he felt a muscle tear and was in some pain when he got back to his office. As the pain grew worse, he telephoned me and I agreed to see him that evening. After we'd had a cup of tea, he sat on a chair in my front room and I simply pointed my fingers at his neck, and touched it gently. Apparently his neck became very hot where my fingers touched it, and after a few minutes the pain disappeared and did not return.

On another occasion, after a game of squash, there seemed to be some problem at the base of his spine which caused greater and greater muscular discomfort. Sitting or lying down for any length of time only exacerbated the problem.

I was due to have dinner with my friends and saw what the trouble was. After dinner I performed directional healing, and the pain and discomfort gradually and totally disappeared. This was done as we carried on our normal conversation, with no physical manipulation or laying-on of hands in any way. It was possible to use directional healing in this case as I was sure of a good response from my subject, who had already experienced my healing powers. Although I do healing, it is sometimes necessary to bolster people's confidence and co-operation in the healing process by the laying-on of hands.

And it isn't only people I've been able to help. Once I was asked to help a dog, and as a dog-lover how could I refuse? An office colleague of a friend seemed to be becoming increasingly depressed. Eventually my friend enquired why and learnt that his colleague's St Bernard puppy, Bruno, had parvo-virus and was not expected to survive. My friend had lunch with his colleague then called me. The next day the dog's owner looked a changed man. Apparently, after lunchtime the previous day, Bruno had begun to eat again. The dog's improvement continued, much to the amazement of his owners and the vet. Bruno eventually did so well he was entered in dog shows.

I was also able to help, through absent healing, the talented organist, Jeremy Wallbank. He has performed widely here and abroad and won many awards. I'd prefer him to tell his story in his own words. I can't help but feel embarrassed when I have to include things like this which make it sound as if I'm blowing my own trumpet all the time. At least including these anecdotes in my friends' own words makes me feel better about it! I relate these cases of healing so that people can know something about the great healing power which is available to all who draw upon it and are receptive to it.

> I have had total diabetes since the age of four (I am now 27) and have been completely insulin-dependent since that age. Since you first included me on your healing list a number of interesting things have happened. Most particularly, the amount of insulin required to keep the body's blood/sugar levels at a healthy state has reduced noticeably. Since having been brought to your attention the amount of insulin required has dropped by approximately 33 per cent. This is an astonishing amount and has caused quite a few raised eyebrows at Guy's.

In January 1985 I was taken ill myself and rushed to St George's Hospital, where I had an operation. Ironic, isn't it, that healers often seem unable to help themselves? However, it was many weeks before I recovered my strength and was able to resume my absent healing treatments. Jeremy did not know this for some time until a mutual friend told him.

Interestingly, he wrote: 'Reductions in required insulin have not been constant but have happened in different phases. I have learned through a mutual friend that the rate of reduction has been in direct proportion to the time you have spent in transmitting healing.' The fact that Jeremy was unaware that my healing transmissions had been temporarily abandoned while I was ill, and that he suffered a relapse at that time, does point to the conclusion that the great improvement in his condition has not been due to any kind of auto-suggestion or coincidence.

Some people respond very quickly and remarkably to healing. Others show only a little improvement or, sadly, none at all. This is possibly due to some inhibition in the patient's mind, or can sometimes even be explained by his or her lack of desire to get better. You get the sort of patient who wallows in self-pity and is reluctant to give it up. And you have the patient who revels in the sympathy and attention they receive in illness, and enjoy these so much that they cling to the illness.

It is also possible that a healer is not on the right wavelength for everybody's needs. And, sometimes, people will actually continue the very practices which are responsible for their ill-health. I have had patients who were heavy drinkers and continued to drink heavily, yet expected to be cured of the effects of too much drinking! It seems clear to me that a change in attitude and habits is sometimes needed before a lasting cure can be obtained. If someone is continuing to poison their own mind with unhealthy, destructive or negative thoughts, it is not surprising that they don't get better. Similarly, if someone persists in harmful activities – in drinking too much, in eating too much of the wrong foods, and so on – their chances of a cure are slim.

Sometimes, the healing seems to emanate from a particular spirit on the other side rather than directly from the central healing force. The Queen's homeopathic doctor, Dr Blackie, who is now in the spirit world, came through to me one evening to give me some very helpful advice. My friend Vicki had asked what Dr Blackie could suggest to help the eczema which had plagued her for years.

I had some difficulty grasping the language Dr Blackie was using in response. 'Epithelium' was one word she used, followed by 'urticaria'. Dr Blackie suggested we should use my family health manual to look these up and we discovered that urticaria is the scientific name for hives and nettle rash. So it seemed as though the doctor felt that several specialists who had diagnosed Vicki as suffering from eczema had been wrong. Epithelium, we discovered, is the technical name for skin. Then came the prescription: borax in the bath ('not a cure, merely to alleviate the symptoms'), graphite and pulsatilla to the strength of six.

Vicki bought these homeopathic remedies later in a chemist's and started to take them. Much to her amazement, the itchy rash which had been present on the calves of her legs disappeared within a few days – the first time she had been free of her eczema or urticaria for years. And, much more to her relief, this year, for the first time in ages, she has not suffered from hay fever and its attendant symptoms – rashes on the face, swollen sore eyelids, and perpetual sneezing. This hay fever had made her summers a total misery for the past four years. When she looked up what pulsatilla was good for, the medical directory said 'hay fever'.

I can see Dr Blackie now. She has just arrived in the room. She says she is very pleased for this episode to be going into this book because she wants homeopathy to be heard about more. She feels it is the treatment of the future, with no side-effects. She doesn't decry other means of treatment but she says homeopathic remedies will often succeed where all other methods have failed. She says homeopathy is a gentle course – treatment for the whole person not just for the symptoms.

Dr Blackie says that we are fortunate these days that Prince Charles and other members of the Royal Family have spoken out in favour of alternative medicine, but there is still quite a lot to be done to get it accepted in medical circles. She is even more keen on homeopathy now she's passed over, as she can see advances coming in its use.

She doesn't need to tell me how effective homeopathy can be. I'm sure she saved my life when she was in this world. I had been having iron injections every 48 hours for a blood condition, but my blood count would not go up. I went to see Dr Blackie, and, after receiving treatment prescribed by her, my blood count increased to normal within a fortnight.

Since she passed over, Dr Blackie has continued to keep an eye on my health and help me when necessary. Last winter I found it a long hard struggle against coughs and colds – like many of us did. Dr Blackie advised me to get some homeopathic preventive treatments, against flu and colds. I've been taking them regularly and – so far – haven't been bothered by any more bugs.

Those people on the other side, wiser and more knowledgeable than us, are still available to help us. Why should their knowledge and experience fade away just because they have left their earthly bodies? By greater understanding and acceptance of the next world we could be using their skills alongside our own newly developed medical ones to make the world a better place to live in in terms of health.

I don't think for one moment that I possess some unique power to heal, or unique access to healers in spirit. I believe that many people have this power or, to be exact, that many people could draw on the supreme healing power to help to heal others. The best thing about the 'supreme source' is that it does not have favourites: it doesn't dispense its favours to some and withhold them from others. But some people don't acknowledge the source, so they don't open their consciousness to it, and therefore cannot receive its blessing. Healing, as with spirit communication, is simply a matter of opening yourself to a higher power.

USING ALL THE SENSES

A clairvoyant sees his or her communicators, a clairaudient hears them. There are some people, such as myself, who have more than one psychic gift. I can see *and* hear my spirit visitors, which I think makes me extremely lucky. But psychic gifts range over all our senses. There are those who are best at psychometry, which uses the sense of touch. They can pick up an object and immediately its past history comes flooding into their mind.

I am fortunate enough to have almost the full range of psychic gifts touching my senses. I have talked elsewhere in the book about Viktor Ullmann. He described to me the awful stench that was part of everyday life in the concentration camp. He described this smell so vividly that I could smell it myself. It was indeed so bad that it made my nostrils curl. When Kerry Woodward tried to hand me Ullmann's score, I put out my hand to take it and almost at once was hit by the most sickening smell. And it was not only the stench sweeping over me, but a feeling of utter wretchedness. The past despair and the suffering of Viktor Ullmann were swamping me. 'I can't touch it, Kerry,' I tried to explain. 'Everything Viktor suffered is coming back.' Fortunately he saw how horrified I was and understandingly put the score back in his briefcase. That was an example of psychometry of a kind, even without contact.

Sometimes a composer might be telling me about a place he visited when he was in this world, and he will describe a stretch

of countryside or some flowers. To give me a better understanding of the places he is talking about, he will somehow
convey to me the fragrance of the area. I can be sitting in my
lounge surrounded by the wonderful fresh scent of the countryside! And there have been other times where spirits have been
talking about their favourite foods and I have somehow tasted
them. I have wondered whether this was imagination or
thought-transference.

I discovered my gift for psychometry quite accidentally. I
had been to the London School of Music's annual dinner and
prize-giving at the Dorchester Hotel as the guest of the late
Doctor Lloyd Webber and his wife. Dr Lloyd Webber was then
Principal of the London School of Music. After we had all wined
and dined at the Dorchester, Mrs Lloyd Webber invited a few of
us back to their flat for some more refreshments. My son was
with us, as were Julian Lloyd Webber and about 20 other
people, including the late distinguished violinist Ralph Holmes
and his wife.

Suddenly, Mrs Lloyd Webber thrust into my hands an
enormous pair of scissors and said challengingly, 'See what you
can get from these.' I thought it was a joke at first, and glanced
at the scissors in puzzlement. I thought they must be decorator's
scissors as I could remember my father using a giant-sized pair
like this to cut the wallpaper whenever he was doing decorating
at home.

But as I held them, I began to get the impression of music. I
remember saying that there was music all around me. After a
few minutes I realized from the feel of the scissors that they had
actually belonged to Beethoven. By then, Liszt had joined me
and said that they were indeed Beethoven's scissors, and that he
used them to cut up the rolls of paper he used to write his
musical scores on. In those days there wasn't such a thing as
manuscript paper, as we know it now.

I passed on this information to Mrs Lloyd Webber, who said
triumphantly, 'I knew you would get the answer.' I haven't
been able to talk about this incident before now because the
scissors were usually kept in the college's museum, away from
the public eye. Mrs Lloyd Webber had 'borrowed' them for the
evening, and Dr Lloyd Webber was always worried about her

mentioning it in case the curator of the museum found out and became annoyed.

I am quite amazed at psychometry, and I'm not sure how it works. You get impressions or vibrations which can be absolutely overwhelming. It makes you realize that every object in the world carries its own history. If the object has been handled by lots of people you may get very mixed vibrations and you won't be able to pick up a single identity so clearly. But if it has been a purely personal item, the impressions of its owner will come over clearly and strongly.

One of the most moving and momentous meetings I have had as a result of my work also involved psychometry. It took place at the residence of the then Bishop of Southwark who had very kindly invited me to lunch. I arrived at the house feeling a little awed at the thought of taking a meal with a bishop, but he and his chaplain soon put me at ease with their warm kindness and hospitality. They made me feel I was in the presence of true Christians who did not look down on the humble.

As we lunched, the Bishop asked me various questions about my work and psychic experiences. In response to his promptings I admitted that I had had visions of several saints, and of Jesus himself. I rarely speak of these visions since they are so sacred to me that I don't want to talk of them to unbelievers. All I will say in this book is that I have been the witness of manifestations that have left me in no doubt that Jesus was the chosen channel of Christ, and died upon the Cross because His teaching was an unprecedented challenge to the self-righteous and self-seeking. Some of these manifestations took place during my husband's lifetime and we shared together some truly remarkable and overwhelming spiritual occurrences. I must emphasize, however, that I don't accept the Bible as being literally true, and I am convinced that honest and thorough investigation into its validity would reveal that it has been mutilated through mistranslation, copyist's errors, and, occasionally, deliberate falsification. Of course, I am not alone in this conviction. But the great message of Christ shines through the obscurities of wording and faulty reporting; that is, 'Seek God and care for others.' The same message runs through all true religions.

After we had finished lunch, the Bishop tested me by asking

me to try my hand at psychometry. I am not in the habit of trying things like this, despite the episode with Mrs Lloyd Webber and the scissors. The most dramatic moment came when the Bishop handed me a very large parcel which was entirely covered in brown paper, so I had no clue whatsoever what it was. 'Take this and see what impressions you get,' he said.

I held the parcel – quite a heavy article – and became aware that a spirit was building up or becoming visible to me. I began to describe him and told the Bishop how he was robed. I did not know the correct name for the tall headgear the spirit was wearing but I described it to the Bishop as I could see it vividly. The Bishop told me I was describing Pope John XXIII in his papal regalia.

The next event to take place was one that caused me some misgivings. I felt myself being taken into a trance, which is a thing I usually resist as I prefer to remain fully conscious and stay aware of what is happening. I told the Bishop that I could feel myself being drawn into a trance and he told me not to worry, he was quite accustomed to witnessing such things and I would therefore be in safe hands if I allowed it to take place. I drifted off into unconsciousness – still feeling apprehensive, I might add.

When I came to, I found my cheeks wet with tears. 'What happened? Why have I been crying?' I asked, somewhat embarrassed to come to and find myself in such a state. 'Peter spoke,' said the Bishop. 'Peter who?' I asked. 'Apparently it was Simon Peter,' answered the Bishop to my astonishment. I felt very shaken that I had allowed myself to go into a trance and that so exalted a soul communicated; that is, if it really was St Peter. The fact that I have often seen a spirit claiming to be St Peter made me feel no less taken aback. Perhaps I had been taking St Paul's exhortation to 'Test the spirits' too literally!

'But why should Saint Peter come and speak?' I asked. 'It was perfectly logical,' replied the Bishop. 'The Pope would be regarded as St Peter's successor, and you saw Pope John before you went into a trance.' I felt a little reassured. 'Now open the parcel and look at it,' instructed the Bishop. Carefully, I unwrapped the parcel and discovered that it was a book he had given me to hold. Peeling off the thick brown paper I discovered it was a biography of the life of Pope John XXIII. This explained why I *had* seen the spirit of Pope John when I took the book into my hands.

Suddenly, I felt very humble and very moved to have had the privilege of seeing him, and to this day I am overwhelmed by the thought that St Peter himself apparently spoke through me, an ordinary housewife from South London. Since that day I have seen Pope John many times and received much wise counsel from him. I was wondering one day whether he would want me to become a Roman Catholic, but he said to me, 'All that matters is that you are a Christian.'

My mystical experiences have certainly deepened my belief in the Almighty. Indeed, they have heightened my growing consciousness of the presence of God. But mystical experiences are so personal that they can mean little or nothing except to the person who passes through them. To say that I have felt myself enfolded in a holiness so intense that it has created a sense of ecstatic upliftment is just so much talk. Words are empty to all except those who have had similar experiences. Some psychiatrics will explain away these experiences as hallucinations, but how do they know? Unless they can actually *disprove* the existence of God, they are not in a position to argue conclusively that such experiences are mere delusions.

My visions of Jesus and some of his disciples have not transformed me into a Bible-bashing fanatic. What is it, then, that led me to accept the Christian way of life, especially if I feel so much doubt and uncertainty about the Bible? My acceptance has come as a result of a deep inner conviction which Pope John XXIII has described to me as 'Holy conviction'. And this conviction has been confirmed by psychic experiences of a very spiritual nature.

My life has been fraught with tragedies and disappointments, dogged by poverty and ill-health. Together with a multitude of other people I passed through times of great danger and hardship during the Second World War. I was born in London and lived there right through the war. I witnessed many of the horrors of the bombing, and saw at first hand some of the terrible suffering it caused. Yet all the time it seemed to me that

God was walking beside us, seeking to restore peace and reach out to the wounded. Through all my troubles, and all my hardships, one feeling has never left me: feeling of wonder at the infinite love enfolding me, for after all I am a mere speck in creation, as we all are. But to God, I am sure, every speck is equally precious.

MEDIUMSHIP

When I was a child, I thought everyone could see the spirits of the dead like I did. It was some time before I realized it was unusual, and even then it didn't just hit me; there was a process of gradual realization during my schooldays.

I remember once the games mistress going frantic looking for a set of keys she had mislaid. Suddenly, I just blurted out: 'They're on top of the cupboard in the changing room.' She didn't know whether to believe me or not but the whole class trooped down to the changing room and the teacher stretched up to reach on top of the cupboard. The keys were there! I don't know how I knew they were there, except that it suddenly came to me that they were, but of course the teacher was convinced I put them there. I have never forgotten my feelings of how unfair it all was to accuse me when I was only trying to help.

Another time I wished I had kept my mouth shut was when I was about 14. Our teacher gave each of us a postcard and told us to write an essay about it. Mine was a coloured photograph of a church in Italy, and on the back it had a few words written in Italian. I read this paragraph through, and somehow I knew what it meant, although, of course, I had never learned Italian. Later, when I gave in my essay, the teacher said to me: 'I didn't know you knew Italian.' I replied that I did not know the language, but she said: 'You must. You've translated the paragraph on the card.' I maintained I didn't understand Italian.

For me, it was the final realization that I had some kind of special ability which most of the others didn't have. I say 'most of the others' because there were other children who seemed to see and hear things when they were small, but I think they learned to cover them up and ignore them for fear of other people laughing at them. I can understand that because once I realized my ability was something out of the ordinary, I felt the odd one out. I thought I was abnormal. As I grew up I became aware of other people who had the same gift. But the thing that made me more readily accept my gift was that my mother had it too, and used to talk to me about what she had seen and heard. Her mother before her had the same ability, which makes me wonder if it is partly inherited. I'm convined that many people have the ability and it is lying dormant.

After a number of spirits had contacted me with messages for my father, he became totally convinced that there was another life and he decided to look into Spiritualism. He used to go to public Spiritualist meetings with my mother, and because I was too young to be left at home on my own, I used to be taken along too. During these meetings I realized that there were mediums who could stand up on platforms and give messages from the other side. I found that immensely reassuring. I didn't feel the odd one out any longer. One day I was asked to get up on the platform and see if I could receive any messages, and to my surprise I could.

One of the main problems with my life when I was young was that I didn't want these abilities; I wanted to be just like the rest. But in the case of religion it was different – I wanted to stand apart from all the established religions and be totally universal so that I wasn't identifiable solely with one group and would be compatible with anyone. I've realized that my psychic abilities have guided me through the various religious beliefs until I've been drawn more and more deeply into Christianity.

Despite my own early experience as a medium, I'm a bit doubtful about messages from beyond delivered in this way. They can be a great source of comfort and help but they do tend to encourage people to go into Spiritualist churches just to try to get messages. They get hooked on receiving messages without seeking greater understanding, seeking truth or seeking God.

And sometimes messages for the bereaved encourage them to lean on mediums instead of picking up the threads of their life and coming to terms with their grief. It's very much an individual issue. People must do what they think is right for them. If they think going to a medium will help them, then all well and good, but if they feel a bit nervous or doubtful, then I think they should wait or put it off altogether. When I lost my husband, I would have hated it if he had sent a message to me through a medium. I would have felt it to be an intrusion. If he was going to communicate at all, I wanted it to be directly with me, not second-hand.

But through these early Spiritualist gatherings, my father became totally transformed. Up till then he had been a morose sort of man, thinking that there was just this life, which for him had not been particularly happy or successful. Through such gatherings, however, he became so convinced of an after-life that he couldn't wait to be released from his body, especially when it started to give him so much prolonged pain. He died of cancer, and towards the end he used often to see his dead brother, who had obviously come to meet him. My father went over to the other side with this brother to help him on his way.

Apart from that one early time when I received messages in public, I generally kept my abilities within our small family circle. I didn't feel that my path through life would be standing on a platform and passing on messages. I felt that there were a few really good mediums around and I didn't see the need for me to do similar kind of work. One of the reasons I didn't want to go out before the public was that you can so easily become a cult figure, and I didn't want that as I am just an ordinary person. I don't want people to set me up as something special or something different. I feel the need and the importance of the spiritual path, and for me that path has to have priority. Psychic abilities – gifts of the spirit – for me must be kept within a spiritual context.

Going round with my father to Spiritualist meetings, and in my subsequent life I have heard mediums give such exact messages that they left you in no doubt at all that there is a life hereafter with which they are in genuine communication. But I have also seen some mediums give such garbled messages that the whole thing was like a bad joke. I myself have had messages from mediums in recent years which just have not made sense.

I had one message once which was rather nasty but, as it turned out, did me a lot of good. After my first book was published, there was a lot of publicity about the music I had received from various dead composers. One man wrote to me to say that during a seance he had questioned a spirit through a medium about my work and had been told it was all 'nursery rhyme' stuff. The spirit alleged that I was on the wrong path, and 'stealing' the music from the composers behind their backs. I had never met this medium and decided that she must have been a little jealous about my reputation. Still, it was hurtful and I was determined not just to sit back in silence in case the public thought the music was a sham. And anyway there are a few other musical mediums around who aren't as successful as me – maybe I was being confused with one of them.

So I booked the Wigmore Hall and hired a pianist – all at my own expense. The concert aroused the BBC's interest. In fact, they recorded it and broadcast it on Radio London for two hours. The music critic commented in between each piece in the most favourable terms, and many musicologists who heard it were brave enough to say that they had definitely heard the works of Liszt, Beethoven, etc. A lot of good came from that concert and the public heard some of the music for itself. None of that would have happened if I had not been spurred into action by those derogatory comments from another medium.

There is, of course, a lot of competition between mediums but I don't want to compete. I feel my greatest service would be to work quietly on my own, and to find out as much as possible about communication. And the music is most important, too. Once written down it is a tangible thing that will still be here long after I've gone for anyone in the world to listen to. As a medium in the public sense you can only give messages to a limited number of people, even if you go round doing platform work all the time. I feel the music is reaching out on a far larger scale. Music is a language of its own, speaking to the world at large, and not just giving a message confined to one person. Also, music has a spiritual quality and can be uplifting, can lift us up above the ordinary psychic levels.

Not only do standards of mediumship vary very sharply, but there are plenty of phoneys and featherbrains scattered around to mislead the unwary. In February 1971 my publishers arranged for me to go to France on a publicity tour. This turned out to be a whirlwind weekend of television, radio and newspaper interviews. Finally, a big press conference had been arranged at which I was required to answer the usual flood of questions and to play a few examples of the music of the composers working with me. At last this event drew to a close but people were still milling about me asking further questions, when a woman thrust herself in front of me and said dramatically: 'Look me in the eye. I am a medium, too!'

I felt a nudge from the faithful Liszt, who hurriedly whispered, 'Do not take any notice of this woman.' He need not have whispered for no one else would have heard and the self-styled medium did not see or hear him, that was obvious. She went on to say that I must not fly back to London, but must cancel my flight and go by ferry instead. 'I see something terrible for you if you fly,' she said.

What was she up to? I wondered. Did she hope to panic me into heeding her? I managed to muster enough French to reply that I was not afraid because I knew I would be safe. She looked somewhat crestfallen at this. Was this because she was genuinely afraid for me or because she was disappointed at being unable to perturb me? Anyway, I flew home as arranged, and have flown several times since without mishap. I wondered if she had some plan to claim credit and publicity for herself by saying she had averted a disaster if I had taken notice of her and cancelled my flight. Or did she wish disaster on me out of jealousy? Liszt said she was just trying to ruffle my calm, and attract attention to herself.

I have had many prophecies made to me by mediums. Out of all these only one – in fact the least likely – turned out to be correct. This was a prophecy made some years ago. It took place in 1963 when I joined a small group of people who met every week in a South London house to pray for the sick. There was a man in this group who sometimes went into a trance during which a spirit spoke through him. One week, this spirit, who claimed to have lived in China many centuries ago, directed his attentions towards me. 'In less than ten years you will be world-famous, lady,' he announced, in a very positive tone of voice.

I was too astonished to answer. What on earth could ever make me world-famous? I asked myself silently. I seemed a most unlikely candidate for fame, and it was a distinctly terrifying prospect as far as I was concerned. I love quietness and peaceful surroundings; I prefer to live unnoticed, a modest, simple life. I decided the spirit was either kidding or mistaken. Perhaps, I thought, rather facetiously, the name of this Chinese guide should be Foo-ling-you. Now I should eat those unspoken words, for the prophecy was well and truly fulfilled within the time given.

There was one prophecy which was made repeatedly to me by more than one medium, and that was that I would marry for a second time. But I think that was a false prophecy, probably made in all good faith by people who thought it might comfort me. It has been many years now since my husband passed away, and the passage of time has diminished any chance of re-marriage, even if I wanted it.

There is no need to list the numerous other prophecies which depressingly, or sometimes mercifully, have failed to come true. But there have been amusing moments, too. Such as the time when another medium informed me in all seriousness that Liszt had told her to tell me that he wanted me to grow my hair long and wear it in plaits, wear dirndl dresses and goodness knows what else! She was a fairly well-known medium, and, despite the absurdity of the suggestions, I was prepared to take her seriously at first. But afterwards I asked Liszt himself about her statements. 'Do you really want me to grow my hair and wear it in plaits, and do all these other things that she said?' I asked rather indignantly.

Liszt gazed at me earnestly. 'Why,' he asked, very much on his dignity, 'why would I go to another medium to give you a message when I can talk to you direct?' That seemed to answer that. I did not like to think that the lady had been making it all up but if she was not a phoney it crossed my mind that at the very least she must be a scatterbrain! I don't think for one moment that Liszt would be in the least bit interested in my hairstyle or anybody else's. He has more serious things to attend to with his mission to help humanity.

Then there was the medium who swore that I was George Sand in my last life. 'Ah, but George Sand is in the spirit world,' I said, 'and what is more she has talked to me.' That scotched that little idea!

All this must sound as if I have little faith in mediums in general but in fact I have met many fine mediums who more than compensate for the frauds and fakers. There are a great many very fine and sincere people in Spiritualism – such as Doris Stokes of television fame, or the late Ena Twigg with whom I once had a very illuminating sitting – who aim to give comfort to the bereaved and to help prove that people live on when they have left their physical bodies.

What, then, can we do to weed out those who practise deliberate deception, or restrain those whose intentions are good but who are deluded by their own imaginations? This would be no easy task since there are many people aspiring to be mediums these days and the tricksters will naturally work furtively in the background.

The Spiritualist movement itself endeavours to keep some kind of a check on those mediums who come to its notice and the editor of *Psychic News* is always on the look-out for the fraudulent mediums. For mediums to improve their standards of mediumship it is essential for them to be completely honest with themselves and with others, and to learn to distinguish between real and imaginary communication. The dividing line between the two can be very thin and only by constant watch can one prevent one's own mind infiltrating the process of psychic perception.

And one day, if and when psychic manifestations become more palpable, as with genuine direct voice, or even more tangible with genuine materialization, the interference from imagination will not pose so much of a problem. When those days come, let's hope there will be no fake mediums to cloud these important issues.

AFTERWORD

Since my first book was published I have had a tremendous number of letters, and some writers have enquired about the spiritual implications of my work with the composers. I hope this book will answer some of their questions.

The vast majority of the letters consisted of enquiries and requests of a personal kind which would keep me occupied for decades if I answered them all. Occasionally, I have received letters from the 'know-it-alls' whom we all know only too well! Some of these well-meaning souls have told me how I should live, what I should believe, and how their particular creed is – so they say – the one and only true one. I should like to express my thanks to all who have written to me with good will. I am sorry that it is quite impossible for me to reply to all the letters that reach me, but I appreciate deeply the kind thoughts and encouragement sent by well-wishers.

A large proportion of the letters are from people appealing for help with their personal problems and difficulties. Alas, I have not the time, the energy or knowledge to come up with solutions for everybody. But I always pray for such people to have the strength to cope with their troubles, and for help to come to them.

It is amusing – and sometimes frustrating – to find that there are musicians who seem incapable of giving an unbiased opinion of the music which the past composers have transmitted to me. I have noticed that when they know beforehand that the music they are about to hear has come from the Beyond, a superior little smirk very often appears on their faces. It is as if they are thinking: You can't fool me with this stuff. But it is often a very different story when they *don't* know beforehand. In this case, they almost invariably identify the music as the work of the composers concerned.

As an illustration of unbiased judgement, I should like to quote from a letter which I recently received from Dr V. G. W. Harrison, Ph.D., F.Inst.P., Hon.F.R.P.S., F.C.I.B.S., F.R.S.A.

> I think I should tell you that I turned on the radio at a venture hoping there might be some music worth listening to, and I heard a vigorous piano piece that I could not place. I identified it as mature Beethoven and it never occurred to me that it could possibly be anything else. I waited for the announcer to tell me what it was, and to my astonishment it was by 'Rosemary Brown'. This was a knock-out, for I had made my judgement under the only fair conditions. . . .'

He ended his letter by saying appropriately: 'Anyway, you have scored.'

Most surprising of all, I think, has been the large number of correspondents claiming to be in touch with one or other of the composers with whom I work. I know the composers help as many as they can, but it is obvious that some people let their imaginations run away with them, often through wishful thinking. I have had more than a few write to me asking me to confirm that Liszt or Chopin or Beethoven or one of the others is in contact with them. If someone is definitely in touch with the composers, they do not need my confirmation. If the contact is so uncertain that they feel the need to have it verified, then it is of little use anyway.

Many people – women in particular – seem to think that working with the composers is a romantic thing to do. In reality it is a very hard task, requiring terrific concentration, which certainly leaves no room for indulging in romantic thoughts. Not that the work is without its compensations. It is wonderful to get to know these great souls as individuals and to share with them the occasional moment of humour or a sense of triumph when some particularly complicated phrase of music has been successfully transmitted by them to me.

To get anything as elaborate as a piece of music across clearly, without any mistakes in transmission, is an almost impossible feat. Imagine the joy of the composers when one of them has managed to convey a new composition accurately. Still greater is their joy when these compositions are acknowledged by eminent musical experts to be not only true to type but bearing the unmistakable hallmark of authenticity.

But, these achievements notwithstanding, I feel that my total commitment to Christianity is the most important thing in my life. I've always regarded my psychic work as experimental. A great deal more investigation needs to be done to find out more about people like me: all the whys and wherefores need to be researched. For example, why communication sometimes fails; what conditions are most favourable to it; and what is the best way to use this type of gift. I wish there could be more research done into the subject in a sympathetic fashion.

The public regards all this with curiosity and doesn't always relate it to a spiritual belief. In fact, I feel I must use my gift in the service of God and my fellow beings. I am pleased that some churches are now looking into this field more seriously. The religious bigots are dying out, although there are still a few left who are very arrogant and think their own beliefs are all there is.

Psychic abilities are part of our make-up. It makes sense to research them and to use them in constructive ways. We've only touched on the tip of the iceberg so far. We must, however, exercise great caution, as, used wrongly, psychic gifts can be dangerous. I know of several unstable people who have become mentally unbalanced through dabbling carelessly with these things. Only people who are mentally stable should get involved.

If psychologists studied the paranormal, I feel they could learn a great deal more about the construction of the mind and its workings. Students of metaphysics know that the mind has infinite potential. Paranormal abilities may hold the key to some metaphysical mysteries. Extrasensory powers can be a link between our mundane selves and our cosmic selves. It is this rôle as a possible link between the mundane and the cosmic aspects of ourselves that I find more and more significant, and want to explore further.

In September 1985 I received the following message from Karl Jung, which seems to confirm my recent thinking.

> ... Mankind, which is in the process of learning to control its outer environment, is also in the process of learning to control its inner life. The latter is continually proving to be more important than the former because it involves dealing with forces we cannot see or readily handle. It is like a game of blindman's buff: as we grope ahead in the regions of the mind we happen on many things, the identity of which we can only guess. It is as if our minds are in some way veiled from us – yet we can think with our minds, and we can think about our minds. Is thought, then, our only means of understanding them? If so, we need to develop our thinking processes to an extraordinary degree in order to understand what I consider to be the most extraordinary commodity in the whole universe: mind itself. ...
>
> Most people look no further than the trivial round and the common task, but in my opinion that is only because they do not realize the vast reserves of unexplored territories which lie waiting for their attention – territories which could yield to them unexpected delights and fascinating vistas of interest. Why content yourself with the shallow, the obvious, the humdrum, and with minor personal concerns, when your horizons can be expanded to include the ultimate nature of being, the glorious stretches of the contemplative life, and the inexpressible wonder of communion with the infinite mind. ...?
>
> Human nature is so much more wonderful than

178

we realize; its potential so much greater than we imagine. The psycho-metaphysical fields as yet so little explored or understood were completely familiar to that great figure in history who, some two thousand years ago, inhabited the earth for a brief period. He could only speak in metaphors of these fields as his listeners were scarcely aware of their existence. Slowly, the further significance of his teaching is penetrating into perceptive minds which are able to see beyond the words into the heart of truth. He came to bring about a revolution in thinking and a transformation in human nature. . . .

Liszt, too, has borne me out in my conviction that the Christian religion should be the most important central tenet of my life today. There is no doubt that he has had a great effect on me because he is very devout, and he has done his best to pass on a timely warning to those who would abandon religious belief.

Many will try to destroy Christianity, and to debunk the divinity of Christ. Many will deny his existence on earth, and metaphorically recrucify him. But all in vain. He was God incarnate. He passed through the world and it will never be the same again.

Oh, yes, his teaching has been mistranslated, misunderstood, and even deliberately distorted. But the seeds of truth cannot be destroyed and by their very nature are imperishable. The great truths he handed down have been narrowed down, parochialised, parodied even. There are spirits in the next world who deny the Christhood of Christ, who delude themselves into believing that Jesus was just another prophet, a remarkable healer or gifted medium. Alas, there are spirits who operate through earthly mediums, and pass on mistaken and false ideas. Some of these spirits even have a following in spirit, the same as some self-appointed

leaders of modern cults have their following on
earth.

My attention and energy are turned more and more
nowadays towards my religion. As Liszt hinted in the above
passage, there is perhaps a great deal more to the Christian
religion than we have grown accustomed to believing. So many
people feel they thoroughly understand it, but I feel that there is
a great deal more to it which is relatively unexplored as yet, and
I'd like to turn my work in this direction. I feel that if we could
only understand for ourselves the essential nature of Christianity
we would have the key to understanding the whole workings of
the universe. Christ wasn't 'just giving us a code to live by
within our own individual capacities, but a guide as to how to
realize our full potential by linking up with the infinite being,
God.'
In some way, accepted guides like the Bible can be a
stumbling-block. The Bible is, after all, an incomplete, often
badly translated, record of some of Christ's teachings. Nevertheless, it's a starting-point. If we could only apply Christ's
teachings fully, our life could be transformed. We could get in
tune with the divine power of the universe, whereas at present
we're largely cut off from the healing powers of good and
wholeness. If only we could all seek out this power we'd become
a part of the fundamental whole, and division and enmity
would no longer exist.
My work with the spirits – in art, poetry and music – has
already been taking place on a spiritual level, and has, I feel,
evolved along rather different lines from the communications of
the average medium. And as many of the spirits with whom I
come into contact are very devout in their outlook, it is perhaps
natural that my future may take a more contemplative religious
course.
I believe in the one central truth. If we could get at that,
everything else would just fall into place. My work with the
composers is only a very small part of the contact that I feel is
possible between God's higher creation and man. And this
contact is essential. I believe that if any human being can get as
close to God as possible, that contact with the infinite good must

react on other people around the communicator. A case of 'If I be lifted up, I will lift all men with me.'

I don't believe I'm being fanciful. I, along with thousands of others, went to hear the Dalai Lama at the Royal Albert Hall. If ever anyone on this earth could be said to act as a channel for God's power to reach us here, I'm sure the Dalai Lama could. A single figure in the centre of a packed hall, his aura of holiness and compassion touched us all. And each person lifted up by contact with such grace will lift others with him.

My psychic gifts have brought effort and disappointment in their wake, but they have brought enormous compensations, too. I don't believe I deserved them any more than the next person, and I have often felt deeply privileged while exercising them, as well as bereft when they temporarily abandon me. I have tried always to use them for the best and wisest purposes. Through my growing closeness to God, I believe they are on the brink of becoming spiritualized into a creative, beneficent force.

My psychic powers have brought me into contact with some wonderful people, and it's been deeply inspiring to see and hear the beauty they have created. But the creating and the beholding of beauty are only part of the process. It has slowly been dawning on me that *being* beautiful within can be a far-reaching force for good in this world.

An interesting recent spirit contact has been with Douglas Muggeridge, the brother of the popular television personality Malcolm. Douglas speaks in something of the same clipped manner as his brother but is quieter and more reserved. Nevertheless, he took the trouble to contact me recently and let me know that he feels I'm on the right path in believing that words and actions in this life are sometimes superfluous; if you can simply *be* good inwardly, you will have an uplifting effect on those around you.

Since I first began my work with the composers over 20 years ago, the evidence that we survive physical death – their original purpose in passing on new works – has begun to grow, slowly but surely. Generation after generation, we will become a searching, questioning people, ready to ask 'Could it be possible?' instead of making angry denials based on scientific 'fact'. As we learn to research into science and medicine in a less blinkered fashion, there will doubtless come a day when research into life after death will be recognized as potentially beneficial.

If we are to progress, we must abandon our preconceptions and use common sense and compassion. I think that the world of spirit tries to contact us not just to prove that there is life after death, but to urge us forward in our efforts to expand our knowledge and become aware of people's spiritual needs. A study of the paranormal could play its part in helping us to understand human nature. It could lead us to become more aware of our spiritual nature; it could help us to rid the world of its over-materialist outlook; and it could help us to take the next step in our evolution.

I don't think I can expect the composers to go on with their transmissions indefinitely. Quite a few musicologists in this life, as well as the composers in the next, feel that they have proved their point already. Considering the difficult conditions under which the composers have worked with me, they have achieved miracles already. In a sense, it seems unnecessary to continue endlessly accumulating music from the composers – especially as their compositions transmitted from the Beyond are so rarely performed!

I shall not shut down completely, of course. I shall take what comes freely whenever a composer thinks it is important, but I shall not ask as often as I did in the past, 'What next? Is there any more?' I'm confident that I shall still continue to receive instruction and guidance from my friends in the spirit world in their efforts to help us in this one.

When I started this book, I set out with the notion that I wanted it to be a thinking piece, to open a few minds. I don't really expect that all who read it will become convinced that there is a life after death – although, of course, if that happened I would consider it a wonderful achievement. But I hope there are a few more people by now who are examining their lives, asking questions about the paranormal, and who are more ready to believe than when they picked up the book.

In closing, I would like to quote a beautiful passage which is one of my favourite quotations. It is an extract from *The Introduction to the Desert* by M. Louise Haskings, and was included by George VI in his Christmas Broadcast for 1939.

> And I said to the man who stood at the gate of the
> year: 'Give me a light that I may tread safely into
> the unknown.' And he replied: 'Go out into the
> darkness and put your hand into the hand of God.
> That shall be to you better than light and safer than
> a known way.'

I wish, above all, that everyone who reads this book treads
safely into the unknown.

APPENDICES

APPENDICES

APPENDIX 1
Rosemary Brown by Professor Ian Parrott

In 1983, the University of Wales, of which I have been a professor for more than 30 years, lost its chance of setting up a Chair of Parapsychology, funded by the Koestler Bequest. Wales's clear loss became Edinburgh's possible gain two years later. I say 'possible' because when Dr Robert Morris was appointed to the Chancellorship of the University of Edinburgh in 1985 he said he was always reluctant to label any experience as paranormal (*Daily Telegraph*, 20 May 1985). Be that as it may, the reason for Wales's missed opportunity seems to have been the materialist attitude of the University of Wales's Vice-Chancellor and the majority of the members of its Academic Board. I am excluding those who were lethargic, indolent, indifferent, or, like the man when asked about the background music, felt that it didn't worry him.

Why do so many intelligent, civilized human beings shy away like frightened colts or irritated bees from the paranormal? Perhaps because they desperately want to believe that the world is potentially understandable, so they invent implausible stories such as the Big Bang to bolster that belief. Some of them confuse the word 'mystery' with 'problem', imagining that all events are solvable. Consequently, God becomes a dirty word; His introduction into any argument suggesting a failure to explain, or explain away.

We are 'just here', according to this school of thought. But are we? Or do we enter this world from another, a spiritual world of souls, spirits, thoughts?

As the late Sir Alister Hardy said, perhaps Plato's 'world of ideas' may in fact really be there.[1] And perhaps, therefore, the creative ideas of musical composers and other artists really have come from beyond by inspiration, as the old-fashioned amongst us still doggedly insist. But if we write, for instance, that music 'comes to us', can we be sure that we're not being fooled? Did we not consciously concoct the work of art, so that we proudly justify the results as 'my music'?

Rosemary Brown is, dare we say it, an 'inspired' person with achievements which are called paranormal. Even more important, she is unusual in two respects: she is quite sure that she is not being fooled, and she is equally sure that the musical results are *not* 'her music'. This, I am convinced, is a perfectly sincere personal attitude towards the stream of musical ideas which have filtered through her mind for more than 20 years. These come, she says, from beyond.

Rosemary is modest when others have been arrogant about the music they fondly imagine to be their own. She is charming, when so-called 'real' composers are ungraciously thinking more of the performing rights than of the notes. She is absolutely natural in a world dominated by the precious snob. She will call a spade a spade, taking no part in the hypocrisy of our time, when, says Peter Ustinov, 'the stupidity of an intellectual is cried from the rooftops'.[2]

Rosemary is matter-of-fact when 'serious' composers are pompously writing programme notes which are longer than the piece. Indeed, she may say disconcertingly, 'Oh, I nearly said that in Chopin's accent. He's standing by me,' with no more emphasis than if it had been the postman.

The most outstanding feature of what Rosemary has done, surely, is the fact that she has been able to write down the music. It has been a laborious business, even though she has learnt how to improve on it over the years, mostly under instruction from the ever-present and ever-patient Liszt, but sometimes from much less helpful discarnate characters such as Beethoven.

She can be disarming in the face of the fiercest critics, even under the glare of television lights while being asked the silliest of questions by the self-appointed pundits of the BBC. She is a very good medium in spite of the media. She is all these things because, I believe, she is basically a good person.

In August 1978, I visited the Edinburgh Festival 'Fringe' which that year included a well-attended concert of Rosemary's pieces given by the pianist, Timothy Carey, with her early champion, Mary Firth – who was the first to record some of her music – also in the audience. Also, and particularly memorable for me – a musician rather than a play-goer – there was a performance of *Caesar's Revenge*, a play from G. B. Shaw through Rosemary, produced by Christopher Gilmore. It was one of my rare non-music experiences, and was most enjoyable.

Rosemary has often visited us in Wales and we have enjoyed many walks over the hills together, sometimes losing our way. I recall that once, when I asked a local farmer how we might reach a certain place, he gave the classical answer, 'I wouldn't start from here, if I were you.' We made it finally, crawling along a log over a stream in a gully, and scrambling under an electric fence!

More recently, I remember a very happy day in June 1985, spent with her and her two children. It reminded me of how cheerful she can be in spite of the many hardships and rebuffs she has suffered over the years.

It is nearly 20 years since I first met Rosemary at Attingham Park, a college of further education near Shrewsbury where we were attending a course, and it is nearly ten years since my own book on her remarkable music was published. Since some of her pieces have now achieved considerable fame, perhaps the time has come for a critical assessment of the various performances. Several important pianists have played one of the very best of the compositions which have come to Rosemary – *Grubelei*, dictated to her by Liszt in 1969. I remember that when Peter Katin recorded it for Philips in 1970, it seemed to have just the right tempo and assured flow. Then came an interpretation by Howard Shelley, recorded seven years later, which also showed a considerable degree of conviction. I was not able, unfortunately, to hear Philip Gammon's performance at the Fairfield Hall, Croydon, in March 1972, and may indeed have missed several other versions.

A decidedly slower (and therefore broader) treatment was given by Peter Jacobs in the Purcell Room on 1 July 1983. This was a recital, incidentally, in which a new and quite substantial sonata from Schubert was introduced. An enterprising musician, Peter Jacobs, is making a speciality of playing lesser-known works, usually by British composers, and it is splendid to think that his name has been added to the distinguished list, which includes John Lill and Cristina Ortiz, amongst others, who have all helped to bring Rosemary's received music to the general public.

There has been no let-up in performances since the time when I myself was actively taking note of what was appearing. On the publishing side, perhaps I may single out the attractive *Album of Piano Pieces for Children of All Ages*, published by Basil Ramsey early in 1980, which contained items inspired by Beethoven, Schubert, Chopin, Schumann, Liszt, Grieg, Debussy, and Rachmaninov – all most characteristic. And then there have followed a whole book of pieces from Schumann, and a collection of Mazurkas from Chopin.

A sad event was the passing, on 12 May 1982, of my old friend, the leading composer, Humphrey Searle. He was also a world authority on the music of Liszt, and a convinced champion of Rosemary Brown. No testimony as to the authenticity of her inspirations could carry greater weight than his.

Although I have used the word 'paranormal' when writing about Rosemary, we should not forget what Shaw reported about the 'normal' in this earthly life. Shaw's oculist once told him that he had normal sight – adding that it was an extremely rare condition.

Ian Parrott
July 1985

[1] A Hardy, *The Biology of God* (Cape, 1975)
[2] P. Ustinov, *Dear Me* (Penguin, 1978)

APPENDIX 2:
John Lennon's Songs

John Lennon and I had been communicating for about six months when he started to give me some songs. He said that he had begun to put certain ideas into them that he thinks might be helpful to young – and older – people today. He's writing about things that everyone faces: loneliness, sorrow, alienation. He hopes that in this way he will reach a lot of people and give them a little glimmer of hope. He doesn't regard himself as an evangelist; he just feels that there are ideas and experiences he has had on the other side that he would like to share with other people.

He knows that in this life his musical ability gave him the attention of millions of people, and he realizes that he could still be a potential influence for good. He wants to use the contact with me to help people, if he can, to realize that life doesn't just end in oblivion. It isn't hopeless, or a wasted effort. There really is a continuation of life after death, another beginning, another chance.

I've had many visits from John and during one of them he confided that he felt it was his real self coming out in the song 'Imagine', and that he wanted to use his music to say something. That doesn't mean that all his songs will have a message. John was a talented songwriter on various subjects and he doesn't want to bore people with songs on philosophy all the time!

One of the songs I took from John does have a strong philosophical trait. It's called 'Love Is All We Ever Need To

Know', and some of the lines go 'my thoughts reach out to find your soul . . . on that transcendental plain.' This points out the fact that when people love each other, they are not really separated, even when one of them is 'dead'. There is still a link and a blending, an everlasting bond.

Look Beyond Today

VERSE I

When you've waited and you've waited as the years go
    rolling past
For that one love that is special that you hope you'll
    meet at last;
And when it doesn't seem to you that your dreaming ever
    will come true,
There is one thing, yes, there's one thing you should
    always keep in view:

REFRAIN

Look beyond today, for another day will dawn,
And the clouds will all be swept away, and happiness
    will be reborn.
Then your love at last you'll find, leave your troubles
    all behind;
And the sun will shine for ever and ever on that lovely
    day.
You'll have peace for ever and ever on that lovely day.

VERSE 2

When there's someone you love dearly who's been taken
    from your side,
And you're fighting with the sadness that is really hard
    to hide,
Remember that you'll meet again at that final turning
    in life's lane,
So keep hoping, yes, keep hoping, for your love won't
    be in vain.

REFRAIN . . .

Love Is All We Ever Need To Know

VERSE I

In a dream I wandered down the street,
And I hoped that somehow we would meet,
Once again, once again, by the gate in the lane,
Once again, once again, where we used to meet before.

REFRAIN

But I couldn't find you anywhere; there was no one
    round; the streets were bare –
Empty home, empty place where your voice is heard no
    more;
And I knew that you had gone away to another place
    so far away;
Empty heart, empty space, where your face is seen no more.

VERSE 2

So I went on walking down the street,
And my heart just didn't seem to beat.
Without you, without you, there is nothing to do;
Without you, without you, there is just an empty lane.

REFRAIN

But my thoughts reach out to find your soul as it journeys
    to its heav'nly goal,
And we meet, yes, we meet, on that transcendental plane
Love is all we ever need to know; all the rest is merely
    empty show.

We are one, yes, we're one, we're together once again.

Just Turn Away

VERSE 1

Look at me and tell me honestly
If you still love me, love me, love me.
Take my hand and hold it in your own
And don't let go if you still care.
Once I was sure that you were meant for me
Now I don't know at all.
All of my dreams are tumbling down to earth,
I can't bear to see them fall.

REFRAIN

If it is time to say goodbye please don't say so.
Just turn away from me and go.
Some things are better never said.
So don't say them
Just turn away from me and go.

VERSE 2

Yesterday we wandered hand in hand,
And I was carefree, carefree, carefree.
Now today we seem so far apart
And all my dreams are fading fast.
I didn't think we'd ever drift apart,
I thought your love was true.
Now I am seeing with a broken heart
That my happiness is through.

REFRAIN . . .

APPENDIX 3
Poetry

BLEST SOLITUDE

O blessèd solitude! How good it is to dwell
Cocooned from all the world in your hermetic cell,
Where never word that's harsh can jar the quiet air,
Nor strident voice the peaceful, passing hours impair.
Nor can the hands that would with busy fingers work
With creaking, clanking loom my pensive temper irk.
Here only peace throughout each day and night doth reign
In undulating waves that soothe my inner pain:
No sound there is to break the deeply brooding calm
That wraps me all around with heaven-given balm.
The Holy Presence fills my soul with blissful peace;
All earthly strife recedes, and thoughts that trouble cease.
I breathe the sacred stillness with a grateful breath –
I thought such peace would only come to me at death.

BRAVE SNOWDROP

O little flower, small and white,
Your little head bowed down so low,
My heart is gladdened by the sight
Amid the softly falling snow.

If you so small, so brave can be,
And stand serenely 'spite the cold,
A model for us all to see,
A tiny bloom, and yet so bold –

Then should not we ourselves take heart,
By life's cold winds be undismayed;
With quiet courage bear our part
Though humble, yet still unafraid?

A VISION OF BLUEBELLS

'It's bluebell time, it's bluebell time!'
The little girl is heard to shout.
She runs delighted through the wood.
To see her joy, my heart cries out.

For once, I too, one distant day
With dazzled eyes beheld the scene;
But now it only makes me sad
Because of all the years between.

For you and I, those years ago,
Together in this very wood,
Intoxicated with the sight
And with our love, together stood.

Yet over me there steals a sense
As if beside me still you stand,
And whisper comfort in my ear,
And gently take my empty hand.

The bluebells all around me spread,
Their magic blueness all ablaze;
And suddenly I know that we
Together still, enchanted gaze.

STORM

I slept beneath a tree one summer day,
Escaping from the sun's oppressive heat.
But then a storm began to gather fast,
And heat-spots hissed as on the ground they beat.

I woke, and as I watched the storm, I saw
How glad all nature was to feel the rain.
How welcome was the storm; how good indeed
To breathe the air that now was fresh again.

Oh how we fear life's storms, the sudden threat
From heavy, darkened clouds across our way.
And yet when they have passed, they often bring
The calmness of a new and sweeter day.

IN A CITY

Amid the city traffic's droning din,
By noise besieged, where fumes the nose assail,
Recoiling from it all, my senses reel.
I wonder what the turmoil can avail.

There's scarcely space for God Himself to breathe,
And by such noise His voice is surely drowned.
It seems He's being crowded out of life,
The while machines the modern world confound.

Oh stop the wheels, and stop the hurtling cars:
The endless crocodile that onward winds;
For if we lose the way of quietude,
We'll surely lose our hearing and our minds.

THOUGHTS OF DEATH

A flock of birds streams out across the sky
By autumn bid to warmer climes to fly.
I watch them going with a saddened heart,
Remembering we, too, must soon depart.

And yet perhaps to better lands we'll go:
To greater loveliness, for who can know
What God has planned and holds for us in store,
Prepared for us by One who went before?

SNOWBLINDNESS

The mountain towered in the sky.
I had to climb it. Don't know why.
God! what a hell.

I strain to breathe with bursting lung.
My spittle freezes on my tongue.
God! what a hell.

I cannot see; I cannot feel.
The thoughts within my mind congeal.
God! what a hell.

I'm at the summit, so they say.
I can't tell if it's night or day.
God! what a hell.

They say hell's hot. That's what we're told.
I think it isn't hot, but cold.
God! THIS is hell.

THE DRUNKARD

I shouldn't have that exshtra drink.
I'm sheeing elephantsh, all pink.
They mock me with a wicked wink.
Jusht go away!

The world ish shpinning round and round.
My feet keep wobbling on the ground.
By sharpened nailsh my head ish crowned.
Jusht go away!

My head hash shuch a dreadful pain –
I'll never touch a drop again.
I'll pour the shtuff all down the drain.
Jusht go away!

I really am a shtupid man.
I'll never drink another can.
I'll flush the shtuff right down the pan.
Jusht go away!

But when at lasht there comesh the dawn,
And findsh me feeling all forlorn –
I'll drink to shelebrate the morn.
Hip, Hip Horray!

GOSSIP

Have you not heard that John a-vexed was,
    For that his horse was fallen lame?
He had to stay at widow Mary's house
    Which made him fearful for his name.

Have you not heard that she a-vexed was
    Not that her name might be despoiled,
But that he slept outside within the barn,
    And all her scheming plans were foiled?

OLD SQUIRE JAMES

Fat, old greasy Squire James
Thought a wife he'd take;
Needed her to sweep and dust
Wash and iron and bake.

Had his eye on little Joan,
She a maid so neat.
Fancied her beside his hearth,
Sitting at his feet.

Little Joan, she knew his plan,
Couldn't help but smile.
'Marry him? I'd rather run
Half a million mile.'

Squire James, he married Kate.
'Pity her!' cried Joan,
'I would rather stay unwed,
Living on my own.'

Squire James, he broke his neck
Falling in a ditch.
Kate and Joan are both alone,
Only Kate is rich.

THE SCEPTIC

When darkness throws her mantle o'er the earth,
And owls begin to hoot their nightly dirge;
When trees their darkened shapes with shadows knit
Because the gloom makes tree and shadow merge;

When cats steal silently amidst the grass
Until they meet a foe upon the prowl
Which makes them spit in startled enmity,
And rend the air with shrill, blood-curdling howl;

When moonlight sheds elusive, pallid light
That makes the landscape look half real below;
When all the atmosphere is strangely hushed,
And lakeland waters gleam with eerie glow;

I fancy then that I believe in ghosts,
For everything appears to shift and change;
Familiar landscapes loom unrecognized,
Their well-known features blurred and lost and strange.

Vague spectres seem to rise in misty forms
To sway uncertainly about the place;
With writhing, wraith-like shapelessness they drift
Dissolving, melting into empty space!

What tricks the moonlight plays, I tell myself!
They are but shadows of the trees, I vow,
Which wave about as breezes stir their leaves,
And make the creaking branches shake and bow.

As soon as dawn arrives, the spell is gone.
How sceptical I wax in daylight broad!
I know that there are no such things as ghosts –
At least, till darkness falls, I feel assured.

RETROSPECTION

If I could love as once I loved
With carefree heart, unclouded mind,
And know again those years of joy
Which now, alas! are far behind;

If I could tread the hillside paths,
And tirelessly the steep ways climb
To stand aloft on mountain peaks
Oblivious of age and time;

If I, without the fear of chill,
Could brave the wind, the storm, the rain,
And not grow breathless when I run:
If I could do these things again –

I'd sacrifice my hard-earned rest,
And gladly, too, would I forgo
The idle ease old age endows,
The chair beside the hearth's warm glow.

Elysium could wait a while,
And let me linger here below,
'Mid Nature's beauty with my love
A fairer world I scarce could know.

CONTENTMENT

What does the townsman know of life?
I pity him.
He cannot hear the songbirds sing
Their morning hymn.

The sun arising o'er the hills
To gild the skies
A glory sheds that is not seen
By townsmen's eyes.

The miracle of each new spring
That life unfolds,
And country lanes fresh-clad in green
He ne'er beholds.

As swelling buds unfurl their leaves,
And blossoms flower,
With thankful mind I live and drink
Each peaceful hour.

Oh! Not for me the city rush,
The crowded train,
The jostling, noisy, tinsel world,
The fevered brain.

Content am I my days to spend
In quiet retreat,
Unknown, unpraised, but praising God
As think I meet.

HUMILITY

A canopy of stars is overhead.
The moon comes gliding from a veil of cloud
Where lately she withdrew to hide unseen,
Escaping for a time the star-strewn crowd.

Across the fields of heaven now she moves
With slow and stately gait she makes her way,
Until with humble grace she yields her light
Before the rising sun at break of day.

The sun, ablaze, its daily début makes,
And steals the heavenly scene with splendour bright.
Oh gentle moon, fear not the posturing sun:
He, too, will dim before the Greatest Light.

THE CONSERVATIONIST

Unsullied brooks flow still
Past narrow gorge and hill
Where human feet no footing find
To tread beside them as they wind
Through deeply wooded dells
Where drink the shy gazelles.

The waters calmly slip
Below the cliff's high lip
Where Nature holds unchallenged rule,
Unspoilt by human hand or tool
In places too remote
For human eye to note.

I watch the stream grow wide,
Its open course espied
By trippers far too rushed to prize
With leisurely observing eyes
The beauty of the scene,
The water's satin sheen.

Oh Nature, hear me speak!
Your hidden haunts I seek
To keep for ever wild and free
That here your heart may always be
Enshrined in pure delight,
Untouched by human blight.

JUSTICE

If dreams of immortality are vain,
And human life is but a transient strain
Or should the final trump card dealt by death
Annihilate our souls at our last breath –

Then we into oblivion would sink,
No more to fear, no more to feel, to think,
Escaping life and death and all their powers;
It seems the final triumph would be ours!

The freedom which devoted Buddhists court
Would thus be gained by everyone sought.
Our souls would melt to nothingness and cease
To shuttle back and forth in search of peace.

How easy all our sins to shrug away
If after death there is no other day;
No just deserts, reward or punishment;
No need to beg forgiveness and repent.

But Nemesis is not to be outdone:
Another life awaits for everyone
Where all will reap the good that they have sown,
And each for every misdeed must atone.

TO SORROW

What might thou be, oh Sorrow, that thy touch
Can harden many hearts like granite gray,
But other hearts can soften like the light
That dawns so tenderly at break of day?

STORMS OF LIFE

West End shoppers, window gazing,
Tourists mingling, drop-outs lazing.
Storm-clouds gather, must take shelter.
Down the rain begins to pelter.
All the crowds, disordered, scatter.
Harder falls the pitter-patter.
Deep in doorways people huddle.
Lovers take the chance to cuddle.

Pavements now are all deserted.
Faces looking disconcerted,
Peering out from all directions;
Window panes with blurred reflections;
Busy streets have been disrupted,
Life and movement interrupted;
People anxiously awaiting
While the storm is unabating.

All activity is halted.
Hopes and plans are rudely jolted.
We must face the unexpected,
Brave the storm though unprotected.
Life can be so disconcerting,
Indiscriminately hurting.
We must weather every season
Though we may not know their reason.

FICKLE LIFE

Oh hapless life, you took within your grasp
My helpless, trusting soul from time of birth.
You carried me, unknowing as I was,
Through childhood's fleeting years of carefree mirth.

You offered wine to me while I was young,
And let me savour first love's blissful taste;
But when my lips would fain more deeply drink
You dashed the cup away in cruel haste.

At length, I met a soft-eyed, gentle girl,
And shared with her a happiness that's flown,
For death grew jealous, seeing me so glad,
And snatched away my bride to be his own.

And now I sit considering my lot,
The way of life with all its good and ill.
What's given us is taken soon away.
We end our life, as we began, with nil.

But when the time to move on comes at last,
And elsewhere we awake from that last sleep,
Perchance we'll find a harvest waits us there,
And all that we have cherished we shall reap.

HOPE!

Oh, be not sad when Summer
Spreads her wings and flies,
And lets the Earth grow colder
'Neath the wintry skies.
For there's a time for resting;
There's a time for sleep,
When the World lies cradled
In its Maker's keep.

The Earth will re-awaken,
Heralding the Spring,
And Summer soon will follow
As the seasons swing.
For there's a time for waking;
There's a time to smile,
When we find Death's slumber
Lasted but a while.

THE EXPLORER

Discovery! I stand here at your brink,
And steel myself the final plunge to take.
Shall I uncover buried deep below
A precious pearl? Or find my life at stake?

I gather all my quiv'ring faculties
To hold their throbbing energy in rein,
While deep within my heart I breathe a prayer
That all my efforts may not be in vain.

The enemies of progress throng me round,
And mock me as I wait the last commands.
'What sheer foolhardiness inspires you thus?
'Why cast yourself to death?' are their demands.

They heed not tales of noble fights men fought,
Of all the heights they scaled and depths they trod
As they sought wider knowledge, greater power;
Of epic trails they blazed in search of God.

Were they to read what I read, time-engraved
Upon Creation's universal face,
Then they might understand what sends me forth
Aflame with hope, uncharted paths to trace.

Then they might know what joy unbounded comes
To those who bear the torch of quest along.
When breaks on us the glorious light of truth,
All earth with music rings, all heav'n with song.

TRUTH

Truth was a string of beads around God's neck,
Held with a thread of pure, unbroken thought;
Each bead a precious stone, a jewel rare
That God Himself from great ideas had wrought.

God made the World, then He created Man,
Endowing him with brains that he might think
And share the pure, unbroken line of thought;
The water of eternal truth to drink.

Mankind was feckless like a little child,
Clutching at all it saw with eager hand.
The string of beads transfixed its greedy eyes;
It grabbed them clumsily and broke the band.

And so the precious thread was snapped apart;
The sundered beads were fallen far and wide.
Now Truth in fragments lies about the World,
Its unity destroyed, its power denied.

BITTER SWEET

As the past recedes,
Should we extract what's sweet,
Leaving the bitterness to die?
Frail in human needs,
Should we aim to unseat
Echoes of woe from days gone by?

Sweetness on its own
Might in an excess cloy.
Catholic be our appetite!
Scorn to taste alone
Banquets of endless joy:
Bravely partake what's hard to bite.

How our soul may waste,
If like a child that sups
Sweetmeats until 'Enough!' it cries,
We indulge our taste,
Sipping the syrup cups,
Shunning the food which fortifies.

Can we but be brave,
Bidding our courage meet
Feasts that are spread with grief or pain,
Self shall not enslave:
We shall not know defeat,
A noble soul-hood thus attain.

CLAY

When you have spent your life and nothing's left
Except the dying embers from the past
Which lend no heat to warm your cooling blood;
When every day on earth might be your last:

Will you look back as most incline to do
To seek some comfort from the days gone by;
Or try to find some meaning in it all,
And some good reason why you should not die?

We vainly dream our time will never come,
But Death each one of us will come to claim.
It lies in wait to take us unawares,
Or slowly may invade our mortal frame.

Yet many live committing cruel deeds
As if they are exempt from heaven's law,
And will not have to give account one day
When they themselves their final breath shall draw.

With Death upon our heels all through our life,
The path of good we wisely should pursue,
But foolishly we follow harmful ways
And habits that our souls will surely rue.

A rude awakening awaits the soul
Who disregards the laws which govern life.
To make another suffer by our deeds
Will bring upon us misery and strife.

Though cynics shrug in hardened unbelief,
They cannot be too sure it is not so:
That every time with wantonness we wound
We lay up for ourselves a future woe.

You plant a rose-tree and in season due
The roses breathe their fragrance on the air.
Neglect the garden-plot that is your soul,
And useless weeds will quickly flourish there.

The Potter places clay within our hands
For each of us to mould upon life's wheel,
And when the wheel for us no more will turn,
Our handiwork at last we must reveal.

Then crooked vases, ugly to behold,
Misshapen souls, the Potter's eyes will see:
Rejected for their self-inflicted flaws,
Unworthy shall they prove for Him to be.

So, cast upon the Potter's wheel again,
The clay must be re-formed with greater care,
Until the wheel of life, revolving still,
We learn to use to mould a finer ware.

Then summon all your skill and use it well,
And from your clay a noble vessel build;
So shall your work be well-performed at last,
Your vessel with eternal joy be filled.